MARCO POLO

Tips

C900290685

D0766259

COSTA DEL SOL

GRANADA

ATLANTIC OCEAN

PORTUGAL

Bilbao

FRANCE

ANDORRA

Lisbon

Madrid

SPAIN

Barcelona

Valencia

Seville

Granada

Balearic Islands (E)

Málaga

Costa del Sol

MOROCCO

www.marco-polo.com

The best Insider Tips → p. 4

INSIDER TIP

Best of ... → p. 6

Almería & Costa de Almería → p. 32

Granada & Costa Tropical → p. 44

SYMBOLS

INSIDER TIP Insider Tip

★ Highlight

●●●● Best of ...

☼ Scenic view

☺ Responsible travel: fair
trade principles and the
environment respected

(*) Telephone numbers
that are not toll-free

**PRICE CATEGORIES
HOTELS**

Expensive	over 150 euros
Moderate	90–150 euros
Budget	under 90 euros

The prices given are for two
people sharing a double
room during high season

**PRICE CATEGORIES
RESTAURANTS**

Expensive	over 20 euros
Moderate	12–20 euros
Budget	under 12 euros

The prices are for a typical
local dish or daily special
without drinks

On the cover: Picasso's hometown of Málaga p. 68 | Flamenco in Granada p. 59

CONTENTS

Costa del Sol around Málaga → p. 64

Costa del Sol around Marbella → p. 80

Trips & Tours → p. 92

Road atlas → p. 122

MAPS IN THE GUIDEBOOK
(124 A1) Page numbers and coordinates refer to the road atlas and to the map of Málaga on page 130/131
(0) Site/address located off the map.
Coordinates are also given for places that are not marked on the road atlas
(U A1) Refers to the map of Granada inside the back cover

INSIDE BACK COVER: PULL-OUT MAP →

PULL-OUT MAP 𝄞
(𝄞 A–B 2–3) Refers to the removable pull-out map
(𝄞 a–b 2–3) Refers to the additional inset maps of Granada and Málaga on the pull-out map

The best MARCO POLO Insider Tips

Our top 15 Insider Tips

INSIDER TIP **Mountain biking**
Andalusia is well covered by cycling tour companies. Enjoy mountain biking holidays and road cycling trips as well as leisure cycling holidays and tough triathlon and winter training camps → p. 98

INSIDER TIP **Heavenly views**
In the Cabo de Gata Nature Reserve, take a walk into the headland's mountainous Vela Blanca, from where there are magnificent views of bays and cliffs, right down to the cape itself (photo right) → p. 39

INSIDER TIP **Among macaws and cockatoos**
You'll hear a veritable symphony of chirps and squawks even before you get to the Loro Sexi bird park in Almuñécar → p. 104

INSIDER TIP **Take a bite!**
Why not try a chirimoya? Otherwise known as the custard apple, with its creamy, seed-packed flesh, it is the signature fruit of the Costa Tropical → p. 44

INSIDER TIP **Poetic pilgrimage**
At the Huerta de San Vicente in Granada, you can follow in the footsteps of the great Andalusian poet Federico García Lorca → p. 54

INSIDER TIP **Welcome to the cave**
In the district of Sacromonte in Granada, you should head for the Cuevas del Sacromonte ethnographic museum. It offers fascinating insights into the cave dwellers' way of life → p. 57

INSIDER TIP **The real thing**
See emerging talents perform authentic flamenco at the Sala Vimaambi, part of an artists' workshop in Granada → p. 59

INSIDER TIP **Sci-Fi in the desert**
Visit this futuristic experimental solar energy station, the Plataforma Solar de Almería → p. 37

INSIDER TIP Howling and prowling

In Lobo Park, the unique wolf park near Antequera, the predators prowl around their gratifyingly large enclosures. On a guided tour through the park you will discover lots about their habits and behaviour – and on the night of the full moon you can take part in a Wolf Howl Night → p. 72

INSIDER TIP Top secret

From the Casa del Rey Moro in Ronda a hidden passage leads down through the cliffs to the Río Guadalevín. Water was once brought up to the town this way – guaranteeing supplies in the event of a siege → p. 91

INSIDER TIP Once Upon a Time in the West

Gunfights, brawls and stunts on horseback are all part of the Western Show at the Oasys Park. The desert of Almería province provides the perfect backdrop for Wild West movie sets → p. 102

INSIDER TIP New Year in August

Who has ever heard of celebrating the New Year in summer? Well, in the mountain village of Bérchules they do – every year. For a brief period the place is swamped with visitors → p. 107

INSIDER TIP Seal of approval

A litter-strewn floor is the sign of a good tapas bar – it shows lots of locals have been there, an emphatic seal of quality → p. 24

INSIDER TIP From rags to rugs

In the mountain villages of the Alpujarra they sell colourful rag rugs. Once such rugs were essential household items, today they are sold mainly as souvenirs → p. 29

INSIDER TIP The spirit of the great composer

The Casa Museo Manuel de Falla in Granada preserves the legacy of the composer who once lived and worked here → p. 55

BEST OF ...

GREAT PLACES FOR FREE
Discover new places and save money

● *Contemporary art*
CAC is the common abbreviation for the art museum *Centro de Arte Contemporáneo* – and for this artistic experience in Málaga you don't pay a cent → p. 67

● *Free viewpoint*
In Almuñécar, climb the stairs to the esplanade of *Peñón del Santo*. It has fantastic views over the sea and the coastal mountains → p. 46

● *Objets d'art from the Moorish period*
The *Museo de la Alhambra* in the lower level of the Palacio de Carlos V displays wonderful examples of medieval Hispano-Moorish art – for free! → p. 52

● *White villages*
Andalusia's white villages are like free open-air museums. Narrow alleyways and staircases wind their way between the bright-white facades; planters and flowerpots provide splashes of colour. Especially beautiful are *Frigiliana* (photo) in the Nerja hinterland and *Pampaneira* in the mountainous region of the Alpujarra in Granada province → p. 76, 94

● *Ronda and its gorge*
A beautiful town, spectacularly built on cliffs above the chasm of the Tajo Gorge, *Ronda* is one of Andalusia's must-sees. Don't miss the freely accessible – and hair-raising – viewing platforms over the abyss! → p. 91

● *Flamenco in Mijas*
You can experience free flamenco every Wednesday at 12 noon on *Plaza Virgen de la Peña* in Mijas, one of the most popular excursions along the Costa del Sol. But only if the weather is fine → p. 86

●●●● Dots in guidebook refer to 'Best of ...' tips

● *Mighty castles*

Moorish heritage, preserved in stone: the massive *Alcazaba,* which sits on a hill above Almería, was once one of the largest defensive fortresses in the whole of Al-Andalus; now it transports you back into the Middle Ages → p. 34

● *Gorgeous squares*

Atmospheric squares and promenades are a feature of Andalusia. In essence outdoor living rooms, they are perfect places in which to meet friends. One of the nicest is the *Plaza Bib-Rambla* in Granada, a favourite Old City hotspot → p. 56

● *Moorish Palaces*

There's nowhere else like it: the *Alhambra* in Granada. Follow the trail of the Moors between the fortifications, the palace complex and the baths. Be seduced by this place of astonishing splendour, with its many pools, amazing stalactite ceiling decorations and forests of columns (photo) → p. 50

● *Excursion to the 'Snowy Range'*

You can't get any higher on the Spanish mainland: the *Sierra Nevada,* the 'Snowy Range', rears up within sight of Granada. Mulhacén and Pico de Veleta soar to heights of almost 3,500m (11,500ft). A mountain road leads up to just beyond the ski resort of Pradollano, but be aware that the snow is only there in winter → p. 62

● *Marinas*

Andalusia has a lot of marinas. If you'd like to try one that's a little less busy and at the same time very attractive, make a note of *Marina del Este* at Almuñécar. In contrast, *Puerto Banús* near Marbella is the epitome of expensive chic → p. 48, 90

● *Historic date*

On 2 January 1492, it fell to the Catholic Monarchs Ferdinand and Isabella to reconquer Granada, the last stronghold of the Moors on the Spanish mainland. The event is still celebrated today with the 'Feast of the Capture', the *Fiesta de la Toma* → p. 106

ONLY IN

BEST OF ...

AND IF IT RAINS?
Activities to brighten your day

RAIN

● **Science up close**
Particularly for families with kids, there's a whole range of things to see and do at the *Parque de las Ciencias*, from a tropical butterfly park to interactive exhibits and falconry displays. Even worth visiting when the sun's shining! → p. 104

● **Crocodile Park**
When it gets a bit cooler outside, the reptilian residents of the *Crocodile Park* in Torremolinos withdraw to the indoor pools – where you can study them up close → p. 104

● **Tapas crawl**
No Spanish person would even think of spending a whole evening in a single bar. People typically hop from bar to bar, sampling as many tapas as possible as they go. Why not join them! Granada is a tapas paradise (photo) → p. 60

● **Refuge in the Royal Chapel**
The *Capilla Real* in the Old Town of Granada is a cultural-historical gem of the highest order. Due pomp and glory are accorded to Spain's Reconquista royals, who are buried here: Isabella of Castile and Ferdinand of Aragon → p. 53

● **Underwater world**
When it's raining in Almuñécar, escape to a different kind of wet: the town's small *Aquarium has* everything from starfish and seahorses to sharks → p. 103

● **A visit to Picasso**
Housed in a Renaissance palace in Picasso's hometown of Málaga, the *Museo Picasso* is not only for art aficionados. The museum café makes for a great break from the art → p. 68

RELAX AND CHILL OUT
Take it easy and spoil yourself

● *Oasis of peace*

On the patio, on a sun lounger by the pool or in a four-poster bed in one of twelve nice, rustically furnished rooms — there are plenty of places to relax at the *Posada Morisca,* a country hotel outside Frigiliana → **p. 77**

● *Floating upwards*

15 minutes to a different world: that's how long the 3km (2mi) ride in the *Teleférico Benalmádena* cable car takes. It will transport you gently from the coastal plain to the summit of Mount Calamorro. On the way you can enjoy some breathtaking views → **p. 87**

● *Bay watch*

Choose a room with a terrace at the *Hotel Doña Pakyta* in the Cabo de Gata Nature Reserve and then sit back and enjoy the view over the Bay of San José → **p. 43**

● *Fun an the spa*

People who love the heat often can't get enough of it — even on the Sun Coast. It's well worth sampling the pleasures of the steam baths and sauna at the *spa* of the *Villa Padierna Hotel* → **p. 100**

● *Alhambra view*

The Albaicín district of Granada reveals its unmistakable Moorish origins: narrow alleyways, bright-white houses. And from the *Mirador de San Nicolás* there is a magnificent view across to the Alhambra. Sit down on the low wall and dream awhile! → **p. 50**

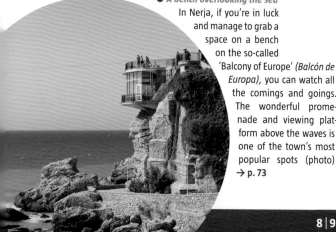

● *A bench overlooking the sea*

In Nerja, if you're in luck and manage to grab a space on a bench on the so-called 'Balcony of Europe' *(Balcón de Europa),* you can watch all the comings and goings. The wonderful promenade and viewing platform above the waves is one of the town's most popular spots (photo) → **p. 73**

INTRODUCTION

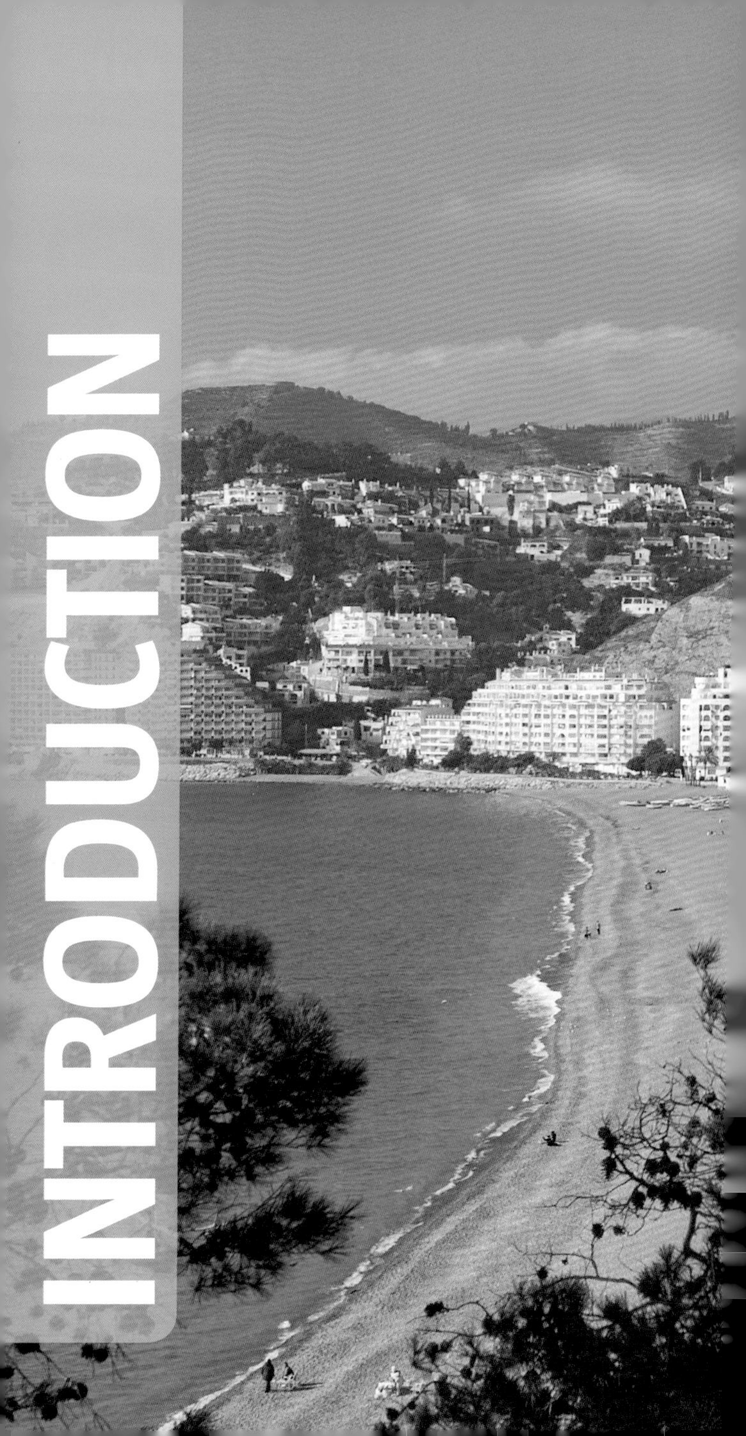

DISCOVER
THE COSTA DEL SOL!

Up and up it goes: the ride in the cable car from base to summit takes only 15 minutes, but it's a journey into another world, far away from the beaches, the promenades, the high life around the marinas and the resorts with their concrete sprawls. The cable car's shadow glides across the last of Benalmádena's rooftops, over the tops of the pine trees and up the steep slopes. The destination is the 769m (2,523ft) summit of Mount Calamorro, which rises like a throne over the Costa del Sol. From up here, large parts of the coast are laid out before you; far away to the left you can see the suburbs of Málaga reaching far inland. Straight ahead on the horizon boats dot the gleaming Mediterranean. And in the distance away to the right – where could that be? A quick rub of the eyes. It might be a little blurred in the haze but there, gingerly revealing itself, is the coast of Morocco.

The proximity of the African continent was a decisive factor in the invasion of Spain in 711 AD that would influence the development of Europe for centuries. Muslim Arabs and Berbers crossed over to the Iberian Peninsula, conquered the kingdom of the

Photo: Almuñécar

Despite its flashy reputation, there are still many charming corners in Marbella's Old Town

Visigoths and remained there for almost 800 years. The Moors called their new lands Al-Andalus – the root of the name of Spain's most southerly region of Andalusia. They introduced sophisticated irrigation methods in agriculture, built watchtowers and castles and decorated buildings with cool, colourful tiles. They also brought with them a new religion, Islam. In the name of Allah they built their mosques and madrassahs and created artisans' quarters, palaces, baths and markets. Spain, particularly the far south, became a melting pot of cultures. Today, the Moorish legacy makes a major contribution to the appeal of the Costa del Sol and its hinterland.

In the Middle Ages, the Moors and the indigenous population lived together in reasonable harmony, but this peaceful coexistence couldn't last forever. In the north, a resistance began to build, its aim to expel the invaders and eradicate Islam. Reconquista (reconquest) was the term given to this territorial and religious war, which,

2nd century BC– 5th century AD
Rule of the Romans

711
Invasion of the Moors from North Africa across the Straits of Gibraltar; Moorish culture spreads across Andalusia

8th–11th century
First cultural and economic flowering under Muslim rule

13th century
Start of Nasrid rule in Granada

1492
The fall of the Nasrids in Granada marks the completion of the Christian reconquest ('Reconquista'); expelled Moors find a last refuge in the mountains of the Alpujarra

over the centuries brought the Christians more and more success on the battlefield. The Moorish dominated area shrank back to the empire of the Nasrid Dynasty of Granada, which extended to the coast of Almería and Málaga. Between the 13th and 15th centuries, there was a last flowering of Moorish high culture. The Alhambra, their 'Red Fortress', was conceived as a piece of paradise on earth.

In 1492, the glory days were over. Boabdil, the last sultan of Granada, capitulated before the forces of the Catholic Monarchs Isabella of Castile and Ferdinand of Aragon. The fall of Granada meant the end of the Reconquista. But the region cannot be fully understood without an appreciation of the historic influence and legacy of the Moors. Part of the attraction of Andalusia is its oriental flair. This also radiates from the white villages, those peaceful symbols of Andalusia, such as Frigiliana and Casares, which are easily accessible from the coast. With their tight clusters of houses, peaceful corners and steep steps, the villages are a mix of open-air museum and genuine communities. Their alleyways, entrances and courtyards are invariably festooned with a riot of colourful plants and flowers. You'll find flowerpots dangling from even the smallest window grill.

Floral colour in the courtyards and alleyways

Culture and villages are one thing, the fascinating landscapes and climate another. With more than 300 days of sun a year, an eternal spring, Andalusia's 'Sun Coast'

16th–17th centuries
Expulsion of Jews and the last Muslims

1704
The British occupy Gibraltar

1881
Spain's most renowned artist Pablo Picasso is born in Málaga

1936–39
Spanish Civil War followed by dictatorship under General Franco

1960s
Economic miracle, onset of package tourism and the first mass development of the Costa del Sol

lives up to its name and is sometimes dubbed the 'California of Europe'. In summer, the resorts heat up in every respect; at other times the region is much more tranquil and mild. The river valleys are sprinkled with orange groves, almond trees flourish on the hillsides, and in the desert areas of Almería not much grows at all. Then there are the beaches and volcanic formations of the Cabo de Gata Nature Reserve, and the Iberian Peninsula's highest mountains, the Sierra Nevada, with 16 peaks over 3,000m (9,800ft). In the winter, these are covered in snow and ice, and skiers take to the slopes. Scenes and landscapes could hardly vary more – and that also goes for the flora, with gentian and crocuses at higher elevations, pine and oak trees at medium altitudes and the native esparto grass and dwarf palms in the arid lowlands. Oleander and rockroses add splashes of colour. Among the flora you might see ibex and golden eagles; a special status falls to the Barbary apes on the rock of Gibraltar – they are the only wild primates in Europe.

> Avocados, almonds and olives flourish in the mild climate

Gibraltar, which has been a little piece of Britain hanging off the southern tip of Spain ever since it was captured by an Anglo-Dutch fleet in 1704, marks the westernmost point of the Mediterranean coast of Andalusia. The coast is divided into three large and distinct sections: the Costa del Sol centred on Málaga and Marbella; the Costa Tropical focusing on Almuñécar and Salobreña in Granada province; and way over in the east the coast of Almería province. Just as varied as the hinterland are the beaches, whose character ranges from the hidden gems of the Cabo de Gata Nature Reserve to the long golden beaches of Marbella. Water temperatures are ideal for bathing from late spring right through to October or November. Rising immediately behind the Costa del Sol and Costa Tropical are mountain ranges such the Sierra de Mijas and the Sierra de Almijara. These block off northerly winds and guarantee a mild climate, in which avocados and almonds flourish, along with olives, grapes, lemons and even mangos.

Unfortunately, the original character of some coastal areas is now buried under concrete. Without any foresight and regardless of the consequences, the construction boom fuelled by mass tourism was set in motion in the 1960s. The tourist industry

1975 The end of Franco's dictatorship; Juan Carlos I proclaimed king

1978 Spain gets a new, democratic constitution

1981 Statute of Autonomy for Andalusia

2012 The effects of the euro crisis, particularly serious in Spain, continue; unemployment reaches 20 percent – 30 percent in Andalusia

2013 Celebrations for the millennium anniversary of the Kingdom of Granada

Far from the madding crowds: shepherds in the Cabo de Gata Nature Reserve

brought vital foreign exchange to a country, which at that time was one of the poorest in Europe and, until 1975, was under the thumb of the dictator Francisco Franco. Andalusia's Mediterranean coast has been a favourite among Northern European visitors ever since. Today, the various communities compete with each other for the best promenades and beaches; showers and litter-free facilities are now standard. Many beaches have children's playgrounds, with slides and climbing frames providing free fun, whether in Marbella or Roquetas de Mar.

Many thousands of people, particularly older people or 'part-time' emigrants from Britain and Germany turn their backs

Fiesta and Siesta: traditions of Andalusian life

on Northern Europe and spend a large part of the year soaking up the sun in southern Spain, enjoying breakfast on the terrace in the middle of winter. These expatriate residents get together in walking clubs, dance associations, animal welfare societies, charities of various kinds, and bridge clubs.

For many locals, tourism is a lucrative source of income, and not just in the restaurants and hotels. Work to live is the motto, rather than the other way around. Even periods of financial crisis cannot dampen the Andalusians' zest for life for long, or destroy their traditions. These include a packed calendar of fiestas and siestas, a first glass of wine around midday, a serious tapas habit – and a delight in fun and noise. Get a taste of this love for life, and look forward to a holiday in one of the liveliest, most diverse holiday destinations in Europe.

WHAT'S HOT

1 Quality not quantity

Going organic Southern Spain grows much of Europe's fruit and vegetables. But now the locals are more interested in quality rather than quantity. Organic farming is flourishing – helped by producers such as *La Molienda Verde (Calle Moraleda 59)* in Benalauría, which also runs a restaurant. They also supply businesses such as *Bio-Natura (Calle Félix Rodríguez del la Fuente, Marbella, photo)*, which specialises in fine oils.

For holidaymakers, there is a good choice of places to stay where you can eat and live organically. As a guest of the *Finca Cortijo Cantaranas (Almuñécar, www.finca-lascantaranas.com)*, for example, you can collect wild herbs for the communal dinner.

2 Adventurous

Adrenalin rush Canyoning and abseiling, climbing and rafting – with *Reserva tu Aventura (Málaga, www.reservat uaventura.com, photo)* adventurers will get what they crave. *Ocio Aventura (www.ocioaventura.com)* even offers survival training out in the Spanish wilderness, and *Pangea Active Nature (www.pangeacentral.com)* organises caving expeditions as well as kayaking trips and fixed-rope climbing excursions.

3 Dancing in the daytime

Beach clubs Beach clubs hold parties not just for nightingales, but also for larks. At *Puro Beach (Carretera de Cádiz km 159, Estepona, photo)* you can relax by day to chill-out rhythms, before things start livening up in the evening. In Marbella's *Ocean Club (Avenida Lola Flores, Puerto Banús, www.oce anclub.es)* dancers and DJs will brighten up your day, and at the boutique-style *Sala Beach (Arroyo El Rodeo, Puerto Banús, www.salabeach. com)* there are parties and entertainment around the pool throughout the day.

Fabulous fashion

Fashion The Costa del Sol is colourful and vibrant – and this is reflected in its fashion. Pepa Karnero's *Pepaloves* range is sweet and chic at the same time. For her urban-look prints, this designer from Málaga is inspired, among other things, by the creativity of regional street artists. In her hometown you can buy them at *Azalea (Paseo de Reding 49, www.pepakarnero.com)*. *Find de Luxe Vintage (Calle de Casapalma 9, Málaga, www.finddeluxe.com, photo)* lives up to its name; the shop has unique second-hand items alongside redesigned pieces from the 1960s to the 1990s . Carola Toca *(www.carolatoca. com)* has a good nose for fashion – which she puts to good use as a personal shopper and stylist. Nobody knows Marbella's fashionable shops better.

4

Alternative lifestyle

Alternative Costa del Sol is not just a long string of fashionable and modern coastal resorts. In the hinterland especially, time seems to have stood still since the 1960s and '70s. You can discover this side of things at the colourful *Artisans' Market* in Órgiva *(first Saturday of the month)* or in the *Valle de Sensaciones (www.sensaciones.de)* in Cádiar, where there are events and workshops geared to sustainable living, art and esoterics. It's worth coming just to see the adobe houses. You'll also have your senses stimulated in *Espiga (Avenida Joan Miró 19, Torremolinos, www.vegetarianoespiga.es)*. Cookery classes are available at this organic vegetarian restaurant. How about shredded seitan or a sweet quinoa pudding?

5

IN A NUTSHELL

ALMERÍA – THE MOVIE MECCA

In the 1960s, filmmakers hit upon the idea of making the province of Almería the location for Westerns and shifted their sets from Arizona, Texas and New Mexico to the scorching sun of Southern Spain. In the desert and steppe-like areas around Tabernas and the Cabo de Gata, they made their movies about cowboys and Indians, outlaws, adventurers and Mexican revolutionaries. It began with the acclaimed Italian director Sergio Leone, who brought Clint Eastwood here for 'A Fistful of Dollars' before hiring Henry Fonda and Charles Bronson for another of his Spaghetti Westerns, 'Once Upon a Time in the West'. Other Hollywood superstars to come here included Yul Brynner ('The Magnificent Seven'), Faye Dunaway ('Doc Holliday') and Ernest Borgnine ('The Wild Bunch'). Later came Arnold Schwarzenegger as 'Conan the Barbarian', Mel Gibson with Tina Turner in 'Mad Max III', and Harrison Ford in 'Indiana Jones and the Last Crusade'. Compared to its heyday, things have quietened down in the film province of Almería and no more Westerns are made but fans can still enjoy what's on offer at the Western film sets.

BULLFIGHTING

Man against beast, but the winner is certain because the meat has already been sold before the unequal contest begins. When it comes to bullfighting the *corrida de toros*, opinions are divided

From immigration to environmental protection: notes about the passion for flamenco, the culture of the Moors and the daily ritual of siesta

Traditionally minded Andalusians get drunk on the drama, the magnificence of the toreros, and the bravery and strength of the bulls. For its supporters, the *aficionados,* the bullfight is considered an art. For most non-Spanish people – and increasing numbers of Spaniards as well – the ritual is nothing more than a brutal massacre that should be abolished. Among EU lawmakers and most Andalusian politicians this concern falls on deaf ears, such is the power of the bullfighting lobby and the amount of money flowing into this sector of the economy.

The fighting follows an established set of rules. The procedure is always the same and after the prelude of the bull storming into the arena, consists of stages or tercios ('thirds'): the tercio de varas (lancing third), tercio de banderillas and the tercio de muerte (third of death). In the tercio de varas the mounted picador comes into play, plunging his lance into the bull from his armour-clad horse. In tercio de banderillas, three banderilleros each attempt to plant two banderillas,

sharp barbed sticks, into the bull's neck and shoulders. In the tercio de muerte, the matador taunts the stricken bull with his small red cape, the muleta, until it is manoeuvred for the final stab of the sword between the shoulder blades and into the heart. A single fight takes between 15 and 20 minutes; a complete afternoon or evening of bullfighting usually comprises six fights with three toreros. Only on special occasions does the torero pardon the most valiant bull, just before the fatal blow. The best way to demonstrate against bullfighting is by not going. In the area covered by this guidebook are Spain's most historic bullfighting arena in Ronda and the Málaga bullring, which can accommodate up to 14,000 *aficionados*; but even smaller places like Mijas are very proud of their arenas.

CAVE DWELLINGS

In Granada's district of Sacromonte and in the little town of Guadix the landscape is riddled with caves where people have lived for hundreds of years. The caves are actually man made, and it all began in the late Middle Ages when people in Guadix needed storage and places of refuge. Over time, whole districts of cave dwellings emerged; today, this may seem like an archaic way to live, but the caves are well appointed, just like any other Spanish home, and without the musty smells you might expect. Between the whitewashed walls there is a constant temperature of 18°–20°C (64°–68°F). Since the 1970s there has been much modernisation, with concrete replacing the traditional packed earth floors and the installation of electricity, running water, TV and internet. In Guadix and Granada, cave museums provide a fascinating look at life in these dwellings, whose occupants include many *gitanos* ('gypsies'). In Sacromonte, some caves have been turned into venues for fla-

In and around Gaudi: the extraordinary cave and grotto dwellings

menco shows; in Guadix you can even stay in cave hotels.

ENVIRONMENTAL PROTECTION

Officially about one-fifth of the area of Andalusia is protected in one way or another, but environmental awareness is not always followed through. On the one hand, schoolchildren go out and plant trees and there are commendable individual initiatives to clear rubbish; on the other, economic interests and corruption often seem to take the upper hand. Apartment and hotel projects go ahead despite the fact they contravene Spain's own laws concerning coastal development. There are a large number of exclusive golf courses, which require huge quantities of precious water. In arid areas, the traditional wells dried up long ago thanks to overuse, and the precious supplies have to be extracted from ever-greater depths. The same principal applies to the irrigation of the swathes of greenhouses in Almeria province, which cover tens of thousands of hectares around El Enid. Beneath shiny plastic sheeting, vegetables ripen for export in double quick time: cucumbers, peppers, aubergines, courgettes, and various types of salad; or tomatoes that are perfectly round and red but contain little in the way of flavour, just lots pesticides to maximise the profits

FLAMENCO

Staccato steps, a pounding rhythm. Love, that deepest of emotions, always lies at the heart of flamenco. There are different ways to express it: in song *(cante)*, instrumental performance *(toque)* and dance *(baile)*. The roots of flamenco are inextricably linked to the *gitanos*, or gypsies. Excluded from mainstream society since time immemorial, for centuries the gitanos sought solace and togetherness through their songs. But the precise origin of flamenco is unknown. Suffice to say that in the course of the 19th century flamenco became socially acceptable, although it was often distorted by the clichéd image of vivacious gypsy women. Flamenco has long been recognised as an art form, split into several dozen genres and continually evolving. Although the gypsies are often regarded with suspicion and still live on the margins of society, flamenco gives them dignity and respect. Flamenco schools have come into fashion. Outsiders can get a first taste of the art of flamenco by seeing a show at one of the hole-in-the-wall cave venues in the Sacromonte district of Granada, though commercialisation does tend to compromise authenticity.

IMMIGRATION

While Andalusia attracts increasing numbers of Eastern Europeans in search of work, and thousands of Northern Europeans, who enjoy the good life in the sunshine, there is no end to the press reports about illegal immigration from Africa. In mostly unseaworthy boats called *pateras* exhausted Boat People wash up again and again on the shores of Andalusia. The *pateras* set out from the coast of Morocco, but most of their passengers hail from Sub-Saharan Africa. All they carry with them is the hope of a better life, but Spain, wracked by its own economic crisis, is no longer a promised land. If they don't end up being repatriated, the immigrants find seasonal work as farm labourers on starvation wages, or in more fortunate cases as kitchen or home helps or in the building trade. Others end up as hawkers – you see them travelling around selling counterfeit CDs and clothes. Isolated xenophobic attacks demonstrate that not everybody has

taken to these outsiders. Fortunately that is the exception, not the rule.

LIFESTYLE

Organisation, reliability and punctuality are not necessarily the Andalusians' greatest strengths. After all, why do things today that can easily be put off until *mañana,* the perpetual tomorrow? To a certain extent, fatalism is part of

and bars all the more popular as places to meet up with friends.

MOORS

In 711, the Moors came across the Straits of Gibraltar from North Africa and initiated a cultural golden age in Andalusia. In the 11th century, power struggles in their own ranks resulted in the flourishing Caliphate of Córdoba disintegrat-

Built in 1785: in the Andalusia town of Ronda is Spain's oldest *plaza de torso*

having a positive outlook on life. A difficult situation often triggers a 'to hell with it' attitude, by which the aim is to enjoy life as much as possible in the circumstances. That applies to the constant issue of unemployment as well as to ever-more rigid restrictions imposed by towns and communities. Sociability is an important factor though there are limits to how and where people open up to each other. For example, it is rare to invite people home unless they are family, but that makes the squares, promenades

ing into small kingdoms *(taifas),* while Christian troops from the north began advancing on their campaign of reconquest, the 'Reconquista'. The last Muslim powerbase was that of the Nasrid Dynasty in Granada, which survived until 1492, when the Catholic Monarchs Ferdinand of Aragon and Isabella of Castile triumphed over the enemies of the faith. With this final victory over the Moors, the royal couple secured the territorial integrity of Spain and laid the foundations for the country's rise to the status of a great

European power. A major part of Andalusia's touristic appeal is down to what the Moors left behind, and you'll encounter their medieval legacy almost everywhere you go in Andalusia – in the architecture, the magnificent gardens with their ingenious irrigation systems and fountains, in the cuisine, as well in many place names, words and geographical areas, including all those starting with 'al' or 'guadal'. As far as culture and religion are concerned, in recent times it has been possible to observe a certain counter movement in Southern Spain: new mosques are being built and there are doubtless Spanish people who, after intensive study of the Koran, convert to Islam.

SIESTA

It is a daily ritual and an integral part of the southern lifestyle: the siesta, or midday break. The length of the siesta is flexible, and depends on how long lunch takes. But it happens sometime between 3 and 4.30 or 5pm. At this time, life in Southern Spain almost grinds to a halt, with many businesses, monuments and museums closing. The reason for having a siesta is simply the hot southern climate. Why work when the sun is still very high in the sky? A short nap enables people to recharge the batteries for the second half of the day, which is shunted into the cooler hours of the evening. Why don't you give this routine a try!

BOOKS & FILMS

▶ **Tales of the Alhambra** – This collection of essays, sketches and stories by the American writer Washington Irving (1783–1859), who actually moved in to the Alhambra in 1829, is a cult read. His evocative prose beautifully captures the atmosphere of that magical place

▶ **As I Walked Out One Midsummer Morning** – Laurie Lee's beautifully evocative tale (1969) about his travels through Spain in the 1930s, including some fascinating descriptions of the towns and villages of the Costa del Sol, which have since changed so radically

▶ **The Disappearance of García Lorca** – Movie thriller from 1996 (also available on DVD) about the dangerous search for what exactly happened to the poet Federico García Lorca, who was murdered outside Granada just before the outbreak of the Civil War. Starring Andy Garcia and Esai Morales

▶ **South From Granada** – A timeless account of everyday life, customs and traditions in the mountains of the Alpujarra, written by Gerald Brenan (1894–1987), who made the area his home for many years

▶ **The Lemons Trilogy** – Three entertaining books by Chris Stewart, co-founder of the rock band Genesis and now an author and farmer living in the Alpujarra

▶ **A Fistful of Dollars** – Classic 'Spaghetti Western' directed by Sergio Leone (1964), who mostly used the desert scenery of Almería province as the location. A young Clint Eastwood is in top form with his revolver

FOOD & DRINK

Andalusians really like their food. Large chunks of their budget and their time are spent savouring culinary delights. If you consider yourself a connoisseur of beautifully prepared food, go to a tapas bar and sample a wide range of little treats.

Tapas are snacks. Although they are now widely eaten just about everywhere outside Spain, they hardly ever taste as good as they do here, in their place of origin. It is impossible to define what makes a good tapa – there is an almost endless variety, ranging from deep-fried calamari to artichokes with anchovies or slices of air-dried ham on bread. The bars of Granada enjoy a special status – as a general rule you'll automatically get tapas served with your wine or beer – tasty little morsels at no additional cost (though in reality they are covered by the cost of the drinks).

No local person would ever think of spending the whole time in one bar. In the evening in particular, the convention is to hop from one bar to another in search of the most original and delicious tapas. If you are in a group, the best way to pay is with a kitty or to take it in turns. And by the way, **INSIDER TIP** the clearest sign of a good bar is a messy floor, covered in used napkins, toothpicks and olive stones, left there by appreciative locals.

Dipping in and out of tapas bars is part of the daily routine in Andalusia. It is a routine that might initially seem alien to many Northern Europeans – as might

Photo: Tapas bar in Granada

Less is more, or so the motto goes – and it's the only way to sample as many Andalusian tapas as possible

the landlady of a small country inn cheerfully announcing that breakfast will be served between 9 and 11am! It is generally a good idea to try adapting to the rhythm of Andalusia, where everything shifts back a couple of hours. Lunch is served from 1.30 or 2pm, and dinner doesn't happen before 9 or 10pm (in fact, many of the best restaurants won't even open until 9pm). In tourist areas, restaurants are more likely geared to earlier meal times (or even serve throughout the day); these also tend to be the restaurants that levy a cover charge *(cubierto*; beware, this is a rip-off), put English food on the menu, or serve a full English breakfast! The Spanish like their breakfasts sweet rather than salty, and in small quantities. A croissant or toast with jam, accompanied by a milky coffee *(café con leche)*, an espresso *(café solo)* or an espresso with a shot of milk *(cortado)* usually suffices. Tea drinkers will be disappointed with the rather bland-tasting teabag in hot water; however, a fresh mint tea in a Moorish inspired teashop

LOCAL SPECIALITIES

▶ **aceitunas** – olives, sometimes stuffed with anchovies *(anchoas)*; good with wine or a freshly pulled beer *(caña)*

▶ **ajo blanco** – a cold soup made with garlic, almonds and grapes (photo left)

▶ **boquerones** – anchovies are as popular deep-fried *(fritos)* as they are marinated in vinegar, olive oil and garlic *(en vinagre)*

▶ **chorizo** – spicy pork sausage with garlic and paprika; can be eaten raw, in casseroles or fried with a splash of sherry or red wine

▶ **chuletillas de cordero lechal** – baby lamb chops

▶ **churros con chocolate** – deep-fried dough rings dunked in thick chocolate sauce; especially good in the morning after a night on the town

▶ **gambas al ajillo** – prawns fried with garlic and olive oil

▶ **gazpacho** – cold soup with tomatoes, peppers, cucumber, onions, garlic, vinegar, olive oil and white bread

▶ **jamón de Trevélez** – air-dried Serrano ham from the mountain village of Trevélez in the Alpujarra

▶ **pescaíto frito** – small fish, deep-fried in a coating of batter; *the* speciality in beach restaurants and bars

▶ **pincho moruno** – skewers of marinated meat

▶ **plancha, a la** – prepared on a glowing hotplate – fish and meat as well as vegetables

▶ **plato alpujarreño** – hearty dish from the Alpujarra: a platter with black pudding *(morcilla)*, spicy pork sausage *(longaniza)*, air-dried ham, fried egg, sauté potatoes and occasionally a piece of pork loin *(lomo)*

▶ **rabo de toro (estofado)** – (stewed) oxtail (photo right)

(tetería) in Granada is a different proposition altogether.

A light breakfast means that by noon or 1pm you'll be looking forward to aperitifs and tapas before lunch. Consisting of a starter, main course and dessert, lunch can turn out to be a substantial meal.

And, of course, there will be wine on the table as well. The daily specials menu *(menú del día)* is always a good choice, particularly as the price on weekdays is generally between 8–13 euros. It usually includes three courses as well as bread and table wine. If a three-course meal is

FOOD & DRINK

too heavy for you in the middle of the day, there is usually the option of something lighter, such as a mixed salad (ensalada mixta), a baguette sandwich (bocadillo) or a single dish (plato combinado), such as pork loin, sausage and fried egg). Similarly, a ham or cheese platter can be ordered as a whole portion (ración) or half portion (media ración); seafood also comes as a ración. A dish you can rely on to fill you up is the potato omelette, tortilla de patata. In tourist centres, you'll also find paella on menus, even though it's originally a Valencian dish. In a good paella you should be able to recognise and taste the individual ingredients – from vegetables (including peppers and tomatoes) to seafood (including mussels and squid) and meat (pork, chicken and rabbit), depending upon the type of paella you order.

Fish dishes are popular but don't come cheap. Salmon comes almost exclusively from farms. Favourite fish and seafood dishes include sea bass (lubina), monkfish (rape), octopus (pulpo) and small squid (chipirones).

In the evenings, top restaurants cater to discerning guests with taster menus. Such a menu, which can easily cost 50 euros, enables the chef to show what he/she can do. However, even though the Spanish love their food, they tend to prefer what is known as the dieta mediterránea: the use of healthy and balanced ingredients – lots of vegetables, fruit, garlic, olive oil and fish.

Quality wines can be distinguished by the protected designation of origin (Denominación de Origen) on the label. Alongside red wine (tinto), rosé (rosado) and white wine (blanco) there is also dessert wine made of muscatel grapes (e.g. vino de Málaga). Good Spanish brands of beer include San Miguel and Mahou. If you want a draught beer order a caña; a cerveza normally refers to a bottled beer, which usually comes in small sizes (0.25l or 0.33l); a further variation is alcohol-free beer (cerveza sin alcohol). Because of the high level of chlorine in tap water, it's better to order mineral water (agua mineral).

Tucking into the tapas: tinto and tortilla

It isn't just the strong dessert wines that are typical of Andalusia, but also sherry, produced in the area around Jerez de la Frontera. One shouldn't order a 'sherry' but go directly for the required type – fino for a dry sherry, amontillado for a medium and oloroso for a sweet sherry.

SHOPPING

Artisan traditions and the large number of visitors make this part of Andalusia a shopper's paradise. In Granada's atmospheric Alcaicería, which was once the Moors' silk bazaar, visitors will think they've been carried off to the Orient. However there is quite a lot of overpriced and stereotypical rubbish: flamenco dancer dolls, castanets and flamenco costumes made of cheap material, and plenty of tourist tat made in China.

In contrast, authentic art and crafts reflect the influences of the various different cultures that have left their mark on the region: Phoenicians, Iberians, Romans and especially the Moors. The youthful Spanish fashion scene from Madrid and Barcelona has also spread to Andalusia. While places like Puerto Banús concentrate on smart boutiques, in Almería and Granada things are a bit more down-to-earth. Leather shoes are generally cheaper than they are at home. *Fluchos* is a top-quality brand – handsewn shoes for men and women.

A valuable tip on the side: in chemists (farmacias) a lot of branded drugs are cheaper than at home. Many drugs available only on prescription in the UK and other countries can be purchased over the counter here.

CULINARY ITEMS

Jars of marinated olives *(aceitunas)* are inexpensive and easy to transport, as are tins of liver pâté made from the flavoursome black Iberian pork *(paté de higado de cerdo ibérico)*. If the service is available, a spicy *chorizo* or a nice piece of Serrano ham can be INSIDER TIP shrink-wrapped *(envasar al vacío)* for the journey home. If you're tempted to buy a complete leg of ham, perhaps in the Alpujarra town of Trevélez, you should be aware that without a ham stand *(jamonero)* holding and cutting the joint will be a struggle. A sweet speciality is sugarcane syrup *(miel de caña)* from Frigiliana. If you're here with your own car, it's worth leaving room for a couple of bottles: extra virgin olive oil *(aceite de oliva virgen extra)*, wine, grape marc brandy *(orujo)* from the Alpujarra or dessert wine from Cómpeta.

INLAY

Taracea is the name given to the Moorish-inspired inlay work that you'll see on jewellery boxes, chessboards, mirror frames, trays, musical boxes and tables. The craftsmen create beautiful mosaics

There are real treasure troves for souvenir hunters – but the boundary between art and kitsch is often blurred

from a variety of materials, including bone fragments, mother-of-pearl and precious woods. You'll find the largest choice in Granada.

MARKETS

Street markets *(mercadillos)* have fixed times and places. Especially popular are the colourful stands and stalls that set up in coastal towns such as Nerja, Fuengirola, Torremolinos, Estepona and Marbella.

MUSICAL INSTRUMENTS

Alongside Madrid, Granada ranks as the most important place in Spain for making guitars. There are still more than two dozen guitar workshops in the province of Granada. They make classical and flamenco guitars.

POTTERY

Look out for glazed plates, bowls and mugs in green and blue on a white background. This classic design dates back to the time of the Nasrids, the last Moorish dynasty in Spain. Pots, cups and saucers are also available. There is a particularly big choice in Granada.

RAG RUGS

Jarapas are the INSIDER TIP rag rugs, that are sold in the larger mountain villages of the Alpujarra. This traditional craft of weaving strips of cloth into colourful rugs has been turned into a thriving cottage industry. Attractive and reasonably priced souvenirs, small rag rugs cost from 6 euros, larger ones around 25 euros. Despite the 'machine washable' claim, as a precaution you should only wash your rug by hand.

THE PERFECT ROUTE

START IN THE CITY OF MÁLAGA

The starting point is the airport at ① *Málaga* → p. 64, where there are plenty of car hire companies. Because it lies to the southwest of the city, stay on that side for the moment and make your first acquaintance with the coast at ② *Benalmádena* → p. 86. In the evening, take in the atmosphere around the marina.

HEADING EAST

On the following day, drive around the perimeter of the city and head for one of the highlights of the eastern Costa del Sol, the town of ③ *Nerja* → p. 73. Everyone visits the 'Balcony of Europe', but the string of small beaches and the famous caves are also worth closer inspection. You can also take a detour into the mountains to one of the most picturesque villages in Southern Spain, ④ *Frigiliana* → p. 76. Stay the night here or go on to ⑤ *Almuñécar* → p. 45 (photo above), the capital of the Costa Tropical. The journey continues east via picturesque ⑥ *Salobreña* → p. 48 and then through a gleaming, almost surreal world of plastic greenhouses to ⑦ *Almería* → p. 32, with its gigantic Moorish castle. Break your journey here, then continue to the Cabo de Gata Nature Reserve for two nights in the little town of ⑧ *San José* → p. 41. During the daytime you can discover the little beaches to the southwest as well as the wild coastal scenery. The crystal-clear water is sure to tempt you in for a dip!

OFF TO GRANADA!

You can now wave goodbye to the sea for a while, and sample the semi-desert of the ⑨ *Desierto de Tabernas* → p. 36 and ⑩ *Guadix* → p. 61, with its intriguing cave-dwellings. The A92 continues over the 1,380m (4,528ft) high Puerto de la Mora on its way to ⑪ *Granada* → p. 49. It is recommended that you organise your visit to the city in advance: a hotel for three nights (preferably with its own parking) and tickets for the Alhambra (they will specify a time slot for your visit). Granada is a magical place – even if the outskirts of the city, with their unattractive residential districts, leave a lot to be desired. Allow enough time for a lengthy tour of the Moorish palace, plus time to sample the tapas bars, stroll around the old city, see the Royal Chapel and the Cathedral, and explore the labyrinthine district of the Albaicín.

Experience the variety of the Costa del Sol with this trip to the Cabo de Gata Nature Reserve, the Moorish city of Granada and the mountain town of Ronda

TO MAGICAL RONDA

To the west of Granada, the motorway will take you to ⑫ *Antequera* → p. 71. It is known for its dolmen (burial mounds), but the castle is also worth a visit. Further to the southwest you'll finally arrive in ⑬ *Ronda* → p. 91, another of Andalusia's magical destinations. The little town is literally split in two by the mighty Tajo gorge, created over the millennia by the Río Guadalevín carving through the rock.

BETWEEN MOUNTAINS AND SEA

After one or two nights in Ronda, follow the winding road out of the mountains via hilltop villages such as ⑭ *Casares* → p. 83 and down to the western Costa del Sol, where the first destination to recommend is ⑮ *Estepona* → p. 80 (photo below). The next stop is the legendary ⑯ *Marbella* → p. 88. Don't be put off by the heavily built-up suburbs or the dubious reputation of this jet-set destination, but go right in to the attractive Old Town and stay there for at least one night.

AT THE HEART OF THE SUN COAST

The route slowly brings you back to the starting point via the holiday resorts of ⑰ *Fuengirola* → p. 84 and ⑱ *Torremolinos* → p. 77. Don't miss a detour to the much-visited ⑲ *Mijas* → p. 87 high above the coast. Back in Málaga you'll hopefully still have enough energy left for exploring the Old Town and the Picasso Museum.

Approx. 1000km (620mi) including all detours.
Allow two weeks. Detailed map of the route on the back cover, in the road atlas and the pull-out map

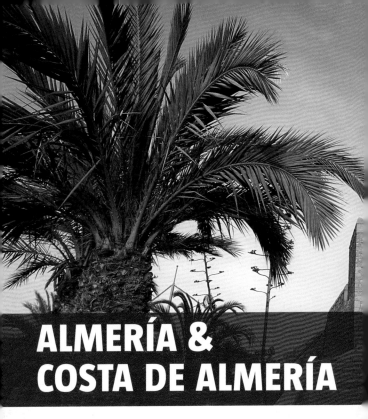

ALMERÍA & COSTA DE ALMERÍA

Interested in Wild West sets and mirages? Rocky landscapes in shades of brown and ochre, rugged mountains dropping to the sea, sheltering glorious little beaches? Do you like the idea of remote bays without any kind of development – not even a shack? Then, in the Cabo de Gato Nature Reserve, you're in just the right place.

This is the driest region in all Spain. The light is blinding, the sea crystal clear. Dried-out riverbeds furrow the landscape, the rocky slopes are fissured and cracked. Once a poor, forgotten part of the world, nowadays the Costa de Almería is being discovered by those with a taste for adventure. Here you will find the most unspoilt and deserted beaches in the whole of Southern Spain. Deserted also means

there is little in the way of infrastructure. A good base is the coastal town and port of San José, the starting point for hikes, mountain bike tours and dusty tracks leading to beautiful beaches.

In complete contrast to this wild scenery is the area around El Ejido, the centre of extensive plastic greenhouse cultivation and the built-up parts of the coast around Aguadulce and Roquetas de Mar. The largest city is Almería, the provincial capital, where the last remnants of those arid mountains disappear into the sea.

ALMERÍA

(129 D5) *(Ω M5)* **Al-Mariyya, 'Mirror of the Sea', is the name the Moors gave to**

Semi-desert, arid mountains, summer heat: the sun-baked province of Almería is like an outpost of Africa in Europe

🏙 **WHERE TO START?**

Obviously it has to be the omnipresent **Alcazaba!** It's best reached on foot. Buses and trains arrive at the Estación Intermodal (Plaza de la Estación); from there it's about 1km (0.5mi) to the edge of the centre. There are conveniently located car parks on Plaza López Falcón, Plaza de San Pedro and Avenida Federico García Lorca.

the capital (pop. 185,000) of the province of Almería.

In the mid-10th century Caliph Abd ar-Rahman III ordered the construction of the Alcazaba fortress. Perfectly situated to guard the port and trading base, it sits imperiously on a hill above the Old Town, baring its teeth of battlements. Prickly pears cling to the cliffs and climb the partly restored ramparts, which extend to the neighbouring hill of San Cristóbal. This is one of the largest medieval fortresses in Spain. Christian

The town hall on Almería's Plaza de la Constitución

troops recaptured it from the Moors in 1489.

In present-day Almería, rings of faceless tower blocks surround the Old Town, but that doesn't seem to impinge too much on the local lifestyle. In the early evening, the Almerienses congregate on the city's small squares, in the tapas bars and along the beach promenade just out of town. Be aware that Almería can't be compared with the region's other cities in terms of atmosphere or sights. The castle, the cathedral and the bars, where the tapas come free with your drinks, are the only real attractions.

SIGHTSEEING

ALCAZABA ★ ● ⚘

The entrance to the 10th-century Moorish citadel leads up a zig-zag ramp and through the horseshoe Gate of Justice, the *Puerta de la Justicia,* beyond which is an expansive area of ramparts, towers and terraced gardens. Historians estimate that the gigantic complex could house up to 20,000 people. On clear days, you can see more than 50km (30mi) out to sea; even though no more enemies can be expected from that direction, the stunning views across the glistening vastness of the Mediterranean still fascinates visitors. Between the citadel and sea stand old town houses, roof terraces and the port with its cold stores and loading cranes.

In the gardens of the castle precinct, cypresses and palm trees cast their shadows, and fountains and water channels deliver their coolness to peaceful corners. Hedges and flowerbeds are beautifully tended. A second wall protected the central fortress, but little remains of that now. The Christian conquerors constructed their own castle at the highest point of the Alcazaba at the beginning of the 16th century – a symbol of the triumph over Islam crowned by the Tower of Hom-

age, the *Torre del Homenaje. Sun 9am–3pm, Tues–Sat April–Sept 9am–8.30pm, Oct–March 9am–6.30pm | entrance via Calle Almanzor*

OLD TOWN

The Old Town has a provincial, almost village atmosphere, seemingly without any clear plan. There isn't a main square as such; the main landmark is the stout *Catedral* on Plaza de la Catedral with its symmetrically arranged palm trees. Skirting the Old Town to the east is the Paseo de Almería, with its many shops as well as considerable amount of traffic. The pedestrian zone around Calle de las Tiendas doesn't stretch very far. Along that street the side entrance to the *Iglesia de Santiago*, flanked by columns, is worth a look. It depicts St James as the slayer of Moors *(Matamoros)* – he is said to have appeared to Christian fighters during a battle in the Middle Ages and led them to victory against the enemies of the faith.

CATHEDRAL

After the recapture of Almería from the Moors in 1489, another menace soon appeared from across the sea – Barbary corsairs. With the constant fear of attack from these pirates, the cathedral was built as a fortified structure, as low as possible, battlemented and with hardly any windows – from the outside it looks more like a castle than a church. Begun in the 16th century, work on the cathedral continued into the 18th century and produced a mix of Gothic, Renaissance and Baroque styles. The defensive character of the building continues in the elongated interior, where the lights on the walls resemble torches. At the east end, however, the ambulatory behind the altar has exquisite star vaulting. *Mon–Fri 10am–2pm and 4–5pm, Sat 10am–2pm | Plaza de la Catedral*

FOOD & DRINK

CLUB DE MAR

Behind the marina, steps lead up to this spacious restaurant, which has windows looking out over the harbour. The culinary emphasis is on fish and seafood. *Closed Tue | Playa de las Almadrabillas 1 | tel. 950 23 50 48 | www.rcmalmeria. com | Moderate–Expensive*

TAPAS

Traditional tapas bars include the *Bar Quinto Toro I (Calle Juan Leal 6)* and the *Casa Puga (Calle Jovellanos 7),* where hams hang from the ceiling. In places like this, they follow the custom of serving free tapas with beer and wine. However, they're not really 'free' as the

MARCO POLO HIGHLIGHTS

★ **Alcazaba in Almería**
Between battlements, towers and garden terraces – under the spell of this 1,000-year-old castle → p. 34

★ **Desierto de Tabernas**
Dramatic landscapes straight out of a Western – the desert of Tabernas → p. 36

★ **Cabo de Gata Nature Reserve**
Volcanic landscapes, semi-desert, cliffs and deserted beaches – the Cabo de Gata nature reserve is one of the last areas of coastal wilderness in southwest Europe → p. 38

★ **Cala de la Media Luna**
Between two rocky headlands, crystal-clear water, overlooked by rugged cliffs: 'Half Moon Bay' is a dream of a beach → p. 42

drinks are usually a bit more expensive than usual.

BEACHES

The beaches start in the southeastern part of town, with the popular *Playa del Zapillo-El Palmeral*. Walkers, joggers, cyclists and skaters are out and about along the palm-lined promenade of the *Parque de Nicolás Salmerón* until late in the evening.

ENTERTAINMENT

A popular pub is the *Molly Malone (Paseo de Almería 56),* and live music can occasionally be heard at *La Cueva (Calle Canónigo Molina Alonso 23 | lacueva almeria.com).*

WHERE TO STAY

CATEDRAL

Four-star comfort and elegance on Cathedral Square, in a building dating from the mid-19th century. There are four different room types and price categories. They also have a INSIDER**TIP** stylish restaurant. *20 rooms | Plaza de la Catedral 8 | tel. 9 50 27 81 78 | www.hotelcatedral. net | Moderate*

TORRELUZ II

Right in the centre of town, offering good value for money. The *Hotel Torreluz III* on the same square is a little more expensive. *24 rooms | Plaza de las Flores | tel. 9 50 23 43 99 | www.torreluz.com | Budget*

INFORMATION

Parque de Nicolás Salmerón, corner of Calle Martínez Campos | tel. 9 50 17 52 20 | www.turismodealmeria.

org (city) and www.almeria-turismo.org (province)

WHERE TO GO

AGUADULCE (129 D5) *(ⴉ M5)*
The rather unattractive new apartment complexes in the coastal town of Aguadulce (pop. 14,000) are in stark contrast to one of the most attractive marinas in Andalusia. Situated just beyond the end of a nice beach, the marina is the hub of the local nightlife scene, with music bars and restaurants. The old highway runs along the cliff above the harbour towards Almería, located 10km (6mi) to the northeast.

DESIERTO DE TABERNAS ★
(129 D–E 4–5) *(ⴉ M4)*
The ground is dusty and stony, baked dry and dissected by cracks and fissures. Under the steely-blue sky the scenery is dominated by dramatic rock formations with colours ranging from dark browns to rusty reds. If, approx. 20km (13mi) north of Almeria, you leave the A92 to Granada at the Tabernas exit, and follow the N340 you can cross a genuine desert *(desierto),* taking in its features from the comfort of your own car. If you think the scenery looks like it's straight out of a Western movie, you'd be spot on. Classics such as 'The Magnificent Seven', Sergio Leone's 'Once Upon a Time in the West' and his other 'Spaghetti Westerns' were filmed here, as were 'Lawrence of Arabia' and 'El Cid'. Almería became an important movie location, and the legacy remains at the old Western film sets along the route: *Oasys* (see the 'Travel with Kids' chapter) and the *Cinema Studios Fort Bravo – Texas Hollywood (in summer daily 9am–9pm, western shows usually at 12.30, 2.30, 5.30 and 7.30pm, otherwise daily 9am– 6pm with shows at 12.30 and 2.30pm*

3200 hours a year: the sun really heats up the mirrors of the Plataforma Solar!

www.fortbravo.es), reached down a signposted track before Tabernas. Tepees, a palisade fort and a dusty settlement stand out from the landscape; the gallows, sheriff's office, church and saloon create the Wild West atmosphere. The authentic set is well worth visiting for Western fans, although it is quite pricey. *Tabernas* itself, which lies a little further along the main road towards Murcia, is dominated by its 11th–12th-century Moorish castle, but there's not much else to see.

INSIDER TIP **PLATAFORMA SOLAR DE ALMERÍA** ☺
(129 D–E4) (*M4*)
Making optimal use of the climate at the edge of the Tabernas Desert is this solar power experimental centre with is acres of solar panels. More than 3200 hours of sunshine per year provide an inexhaustible resource for the production of solar energy at one of the world's most important research centres of its kind. New variations of the technology are constantly being tested for their efficiency and profitability.

Visiting the complex, which is situated some 30km (18mi) north of Almería, is like being transported onto the set of a science fiction movie. It is surrounded by the desert mountains, and you'll find yourself among endless rows of panels, shiny pipe systems, turbines and the solar power station with its 80-m (260-ft) high tower. Established at the beginning of the 1980s, the work of the complex is based on difficult processes and a very simple concept – to find the cheapest and most environmentally friendly ways of utilising energy from space. There is a visitor centre; *for guided tours (Mon–Fri 10am, 12 and 2pm) contact tel. 9 50 38 79 00 or book through www.psa.es*

ROQUETAS DE MAR (129 D6) (*M5*)
Just like the neighbouring town of Aquadulce, the expansive resort town of Roquetas de Mar (pop. 80,000), just 20km (13mi) southwest of Almería, is principally a package tourism destination. Once a peaceful fishing village, it is now dominated by hotels and apartment blocks. More appealing than the building developments are the attractive promenades, beaches with showers, little groups of palm trees and children's playgrounds. And *Playa de la Romanilla* is absolutely immaculate. In high season, excursions in glass-bottomed boats leave from the harbour. Nearby stands the restored Castle *(Tue–Sat 10am–1pm and 5–8pm, Sun 11am–1pm),* dating from the 16th century and now hosting temporary exhibitions. Concerts are held in the modern *Teatro-Auditorio.* Families with children will want

to head for the *Aquarium (June–Sept daily 10am–9pm, Oct–May Mon–Fri 10am–6pm, Sat/Sun 10am–7pm | www.aquarium roquetas.com)* and in summer to the adjoining Aquapark (see the 'Travel with Kids' chapter), *www.roquetasdemar.com*

CABO DE GATA NATURE RESERVE

(129 E–F 5–6) (*N5*) **There is nowhere else in Spain with such a ★ variety of geographical features! Volcanic rock formations, salt flats, mountains that are as dry as a bone, and hidden bays are all to be found along the 60km (37mi) of mostly unspoilt coastline that constitutes the *Parque Natural Cabo de Gata-Níjar*. Nevertheless, you shouldn't imagine it being completely isolated.**
Coming from the direction of Almería or the A7, which skirts the northern edge of the reserve, you will hardly be able to differentiate the access roads; only the signs indicate the edge of the Parque Natural. Spread across the 500 sq km (200 sq mi) reserve, a quarter of which is a marine reserve, are villages, farms, and a network of minor roads. You need to have your own car to explore. The best base is San José, though it's important to note that much of the accommodation closes down during the winter.
Officially, the reserve is called Cabo de Gata-Níjar, but the community name of Níjar is usually left off because its main centre lies outside the reserve boundary In the south, the Cabo de Gata, a rugged headland, juts out into the sea. Geologi cally the region was formed during sev eral volcanic phases that occurred be tween 6 and 15 million years ago. Ash

LOW BUDGET

▶ Bicycles can be hired cheaply in San José through *Deportes Media Luna (Calle del Puerto 7 | tel. 9 50 38 04 62 | www.deportesmedia luna.com).* Half a day costs 8 euros, a whole day 13 euros (10 euros a day for four days and over).

▶ In Almería, citizens of the EU have free admission to the Alcazaba and *Museo Arqueológico (Tue 2.30–8.30pm, Wed–Sat 9am–8.30pm, Sun 9am–2.30pm | Carretera de Ronda 91).* Also free is entry to the exhibitions of the *Andalusian Centre of Photography (Centro Andaluz de la Fotografía | daily 11am–2pm and 5.30–9.30pm | Calle Pintor Díaz Molina 9 | www.centroandaluzdelafotografia.es).*

cones, lava flows and the typical cone-shaped hills such as the Morrón de los Genoveses, which rises above the bay of the same name, are a legacy of this long gone era of volcanism.

Even though greenhouses come right up to the edge of the reserve, a series of fortunate circumstances has protected the coastal strip from greater inundation from agriculture and tourism. Intriguingly, pirates can be regarded as the founding fathers of the reserve. The constant threat from the sea saw to it that the coast remained largely free of settlement, other than some minor defences constructed during the 18th century. The barren mountains and hills, which reach all the way to the beaches, have a steppe and semi-desert character. Half an hour of rain in November is treated as a major event here; between April and October there is normally no rain at all. Only the nightly mist delivers enough moisture to enable small bushes of herbs, esparto grass and dwarf palms to survive.

PLACES IN THE NATURE RESERVE

CABO DE GATA ☆ (129 E6) (*N5*)

Vertical cliffs, a lighthouse and churning seas – Cabo de Gata has all the classic features of a cape, but even more spectacular and magical is the neighbouring formation of *Arrecife de las Sirenas,* the 'Mermaid's Reef', whose rocks rise out of the sea like needles. This is a mini maritime mountain range, the remnants of a volcanic chimney. Until the mid-20th century it was home to colonies of monk seals, the origin of the 'mermaids' in the name. According to superstition among local fishermen, the sounds they heard were not produced by these animals at all, but by mermaids.

The only road to the cape leads from the little village of *San Miguel de Cabo de Gata* (often just called El Cabo de Gata), where there is a small promenade and old watchtower in the sand, down the flat western section of the reserve via La Almadraba de Monteleva. Either side of

A lighthouse and rugged cliffs: Cabo de Gata is a classic cape

San Miguel a pebbly beach stretches away for more than a kilometre. Evidence that salt is still being extracted from the local flats is provided by the mounds near the side of the road just before La Almadraba.

A detour from the cape into the ☆ INSIDER TIP *Vela Blanca* hills provides the best views in the reserve. Whether you're here by car or on foot, you get there as follows: some 300m/yds before the car park at the cape, take the incon-

CABO DE GATA NATURE RESERVE

The little resort of La Isleta del Moro lies on the neck of a peninsula

spicuous little road to the left past the Aula del Mar information centre, dwarf palms and the car park above the bay of Cala Rajá. Beyond, the road winds its way into the hills for 1.6km (1mi), where the historic watchtower of Vela Blanca and a modern radio transmitter act as beacons. The road ends at the transmitter – with wonderful views of the cape. At your feet, below the nearby watchtower, is the east coast of the reserve, studded with bays, leading towards San José. The track going down to beaches and bays such as Cala de la Media Luna is closed to motor traffic but not to mountain-bikers or hikers. Because of the wide inland loop motorists still have another 30km (19mi) from the Cape to San José.

LA ISLETA DEL MORO ☼
(129 E5–6) (*𝑚 N5*)
The little resort and fishing village not far from Pozo de los Frailes sits on the neck of a headland jutting into the sea. There is a beautiful view across the bay to the Frailes Massif.

RODALQUILAR (129 E5) (*𝑚 N5*)
The eerie shells of abandoned buildings and deserted ponds at the edge of this village recall the days when there was a gold rush in these parts. Gold was discovered here in 1883, and it was a British mining company that first exploited the rich seams. Hundreds of workers were employed in the mines right up until the 1950s. But by 1966 all the seams had been worked out. 'Minas de Oro' signs in the centre of the village direct you to the concrete ruins. There is also a small museum on site. On the approach to the village, beautiful views of the coast open up from the ☼ *Mirador Las Amatistas* viewpoint.

INFORMATION

The Nature Reserve Visitor Centre lies a few kilometres northeast of San Miguel near Ruescas/Rambla de Morales; the route there is clearly signposted. *Centro de Visitantes Las Amoladeras | tel. 9 50 16 04 35*

SAN JOSÉ

(129 E6) (🗺 N5) **Several small hotels and restaurants make San José (pop. 2,000) the largest and most convenient base for exploring the Cabo de Gata Nature Reserve.**

San José is situated on a broad bay on the east coast of the nature reserve. Its brilliant white houses stretch just a short distance inland, for the bay is dominated by the rugged foothills of the Sierra de Cabo de Gata including the 500m (1,640ft) high Frailes Massif. It is a cul-de sac at the southern end of the only access road from inland (via El Pozo de los Frailes). After that, a single track leads southwest to beautiful beaches such as Los Genoveses and Media Luna. This track is accessible by car (if you're hiring a car check in advance the terms and conditions in the hire agreement to ensure you can go off road) as well as mountain bike. In San José itself, life revolves around the Plaza de Génova, with its palm trees, the Paseo Marítimo beach promenade and motorboat and yacht marina.

FOOD & DRINK

LA CUEVA DE ANTONIO

Among the seafood specialities are octopus salad and fresh shrimps. It has a large terraced area right on the beach promenade. *In high summer daily, otherwise closed Wed | Paseo Marítimo 37 | tel. 9 50 38 01 54 | Budget–Moderate*

LA TABERNA DEL PUERTO

Good *calamares* and grilled lamb chops are on the menu at this quayside restaurant at the harbour. There are also other good restaurants in the vicinity. *Closed Wed | Puerto Deportivo | tel. 9 50 38 00 42 | Moderate*

BEACHES

From the southwest end of San José a track runs parallel to the coast for approx. 8km (5mi); along the way are turn-offs to the beach car parks. In summer, when large numbers of visitors come to the beaches, and the car parks fill up quickly, a shuttle bus service is sometimes laid on from San José; the procedure changes from summer to summer, so it's difficult to predict when this will be the case. Out-

BIRDWATCHING

There are some 500–600 pink flamingos that live all year in the salt flats of the Cabo de Gata Nature Reserve. In summer, the number of birds rises to 2,500. It's possible to watch the birds from freely accessible hides: just before San Miguel de Cabo de Gata to the left of the road (coming from the direction of Rambla de Morales) or, even better, from the Observatorio Las Salinas on the stretch between San Miguel and the cape (signed to the left). With a bit of luck, you should also be able to spot grey and silver herons, black-winged stilts, cormorants and pied avocets. A total of more than 80 species of birds can be found here, so make sure you bring your binoculars. It's possible to do an approx. 11km (7mi) hike around the salt flats.

side the peak summer months, you'll have long stretches of beach almost all to yourself.

Die *Playa de los Genoveses* curves like a sickle towards the volcanic cone of Morrón de los Genoveses; in the central section of the beach there are fossilised dunes. Between the beaches of Genoveses and Mónsul lies *Playa Barronal,* an official nudist beach. You can get there if you leave your car at the track car park and then trudge across the dunes for about 10 minutes. More easily reached are the last beaches off the track: *Playa del Mónsul* and Cala de la Media Luna, both with dusty car parks behind them.

Enclosed at each end by rocky headlands, the 300m/yds long 'Half Moon Bay' ⭐ *Cala de la Media Luna,* with its fine sand and crystal-clear water, is everything that an unspoilt, heavenly little beach should be – except for the fact that there is no shade whatsoever, so you will need to bring your own. Down the coast towards the cape, a series of rugged mountain spurs dramatically illustrate the forces of nature at work here. The colours alternate between ochre, chalk white and rusty brown. In the background rise the Vela Blanca hills.

If you want to explore the reserve north of San José, the nicest beach is *Playa de los Muertos* between Agua Amarga and Carboneras.

RECREATION & TOURS

From San José, the agency *Grupo J126 – Rutas de la Naturaleza (Avenida de San José 27 | tel. 9 50 38 02 99 | cabodegata-nijar.com)* organises INSIDER TIP▶ Jeep tours and walks as well as providing neutral tourist information about the reserve. A night-time walk in summer will take you beneath the starlit skies of the semi-desert. For the daytime tours, don't forget water and sun protection!

Tip for INSIDER TIP▶ a nice mountain bike tour that you can undertake yourself through the Cabo de Gata nature reserve: from San José (bike hire available) follow the dust track to the south past the beaches. Beyond the last one, Cala de la Media Luna, pass the barrier and ascend the track as it makes a broad loop into Vela Blanca hills, up towards the old watchtower and radio transmitter. Then descend to the cape along a potholed tarmac road. Return the same way: total distance approx. 25km (16mi). Strenuous!

A good hike is to follow the track from San José for a short distance towards Playa de los Genoveses, and at the hill beneath the windmill take the signed footpath *Sendero Los Genoveses*, diagonally to the left.

The target from here is the *Morrón de los Genoveses,* a volcanic cone above the beach 2.3km (1.5mi) away. Beyond Playa de los Genoveses INSIDER TIP experienced hikers can follow the coast from bay to bay as far as Playa del Mónsul, Caution: the route doesn't follow the water's edge but goes slightly inland, passing along sometimes very steep scree slopes and through deep depressions. The path is not always recognisable.

WHERE TO STAY

INSIDER TIP DOÑA PAKYTA ● ✼

A stylish little hotel, where the additional charge for the terrace with its beautiful panoramic view of the bay is well worth it. Steps lead from the hotel directly to the beach. The restaurant *(in summer daily otherwise closed on alternate days |* *Moderate–Expensive)* with its outdoor terrace (booking essential in the high season!) is open to non-residents. *13 rooms | Calle Correo 51 | tel. 9 50 61 11 75 | www.hotelpakyta.es | Moderate*

EL DORADO ✼

A friendly *hostal* occupying an elevated position in the centre. The rooms are in a good state and the prices include breakfast. *27 rooms | Camino de Agua-marina | tel. 9 50 38 01 18 | www.hostalel dorado.com | Budget*

EL SANTUARIO DE SAN JOSÉ

Simple, clean *hostal* with its own restaurant, within easy walking distance of the beach and harbour. Prices include breakfast. *28 rooms | Camino de Cala Higuera 9 | tel. 9 50 38 05 03 | www.elsantuario sanjose.es | Budget*

Dunes and lots of space: just don't forget the sun lotion when visiting Playa del Mónsul

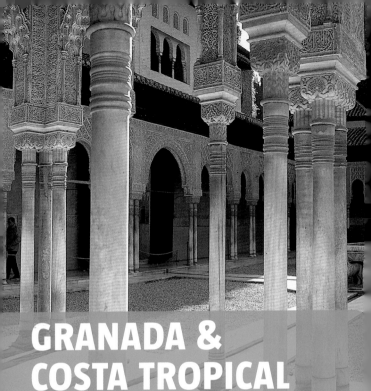

GRANADA & COSTA TROPICAL

Between the rugged coast and the high ridges of the Sierra Nevada at 3481m (11421ft) this region has enormous geographical and scenic variety. And from a cultural and historical perspective the city of Granada, with its labyrinthine Albaicín quarter and stunning Alhambra, takes you on the trail of the Moors. The oriental magic exuded by the Alhambra, the 'Red Fortress', with its riot of arches, arabesques and stalactite decoration, is unmatched in Europe.

On the coast, the region doesn't just stand for picture-perfect beaches; all along the Costa Tropical are hidden bays such as Cantarriján (nudist, stony) and Marina del Este (small, pebbly). A good springboard for some of the less well-known beaches is the little town of Al-muñécar. Here, the beaches are mostly stony gravel, but the water is exceptionally clear. People here don't live from tourism alone. There are plantations of orange trees, almonds, olives and **INSIDERTIP** chirimoyas, or custard apples, as these potato-sized, calcium-rich fruits of the Costa Tropical are also known. Underneath the green skin with its characteristic honeycomb pattern lurks a white, creamy, slightly sour-tasting flesh with lots of seeds.

The other great culinary indulgence of the region is its wide range of tapas. Exploring the city's pubs and taverns is an integral part of a visit to Granada.

Photo: Court of the Lions in the Alhambra

The highest mountains on the Spanish mainland, a 'tropical coast', and at the heart of it all the bustling city of Granada with the amazing Alhambra

ALMUÑÉCAR

(127 E5) (🗺 J5) Fresh air, 320 days of sunshine annually and broad beach promenades are among the attractions of this hub of the Costa Tropical (pop. 28,000).
The gravel beaches hug a series of spits and promontories, interrupted by the cliffs of Peñón del Santo. The coastline is completely built up, a fate that Almuñécar shares with the holiday resorts of Costa del Sol to the west.

For all the modern development, the little town looks back on a long and eventful history, starting with the Phoenicians, who established a settlement here around 2800 years ago. The remains of their fish-curing plant *(fábrica de salazones),* which was later taken over by the Romans, lie in the Park El Majuelo, below the castle. The oldest part of town, with its twisting alleyways and whitewashed houses, is in the Upper Town, between the castle and the Archaeological Museum. Here, plant pots flank the doorways, and strangers

still receive a friendly welcome from the older residents of the town. This is in stark contrast to the hustle and bustle of the Calle Real area near the town hall. Behind the town rises the mountain barrier of the Sierra de Almijara.

SIGHTSEEING

CASTILLO DE SAN MIGUEL AND INSIDER TIP CUEVA DE LOS SIETE PALACIOS ⚜

The castle (11th–15th century) is of Moorish origin, though the restorers have clearly been very busy; entrances and exits lead between old and new sections of masonry. Parts of the castle were once

10.30am–1.30pm (summer 10.30am–2pm) | Barrio de San Miguel

PARQUE ORNITOLÓGICO LORO SEXI

Information about Almuñécar's Bird Park can be found in the 'Travel with Kids' chapter.

PEÑÓN DEL SANTO ★ ●

Before starting to climb this rock separating Almuñécar's two main beaches, pause to look at the Monument to Abderramán I (731–788), a larger-than-life statue that strikes an imperious pose, sword in hand, next to the foot of the steps. In 755, this native of Syria landed on the coast of Almuñécar. As the founder of the Ummayad

The pretty little resort town of Almuñécar still has a small fishing industry

used as a prison. The small complex of the so-called Cueva de los Siete Palacios, which is actually a series of vaulted chambers built by the Romans, houses the *Museo Arqueológico.* As interesting as the stone vaults are the exhibits themselves, which include alabaster jugs, amphorae and oil lamps. *Tue–Sat 10.30am–1.30pm and 5–7.30pm (summer 6.30–9pm), Sun*

Emirate of Córdoba, he rose to become one of the key figures of Moorish Spain, known as the 'Falcon of Andalus'. 75 steps lead up from the statue. On the tiled ⚜ viewing esplanade, a metal cross points skywards. Take your time to enjoy the glorious views, across the sea and inland over the rocky mountains, the shades of brown flecked with the white of houses.

GRANADA & COSTA TROPICAL

FOOD & DRINK

CALABRE

Fish and shellfish are the order of the day at this beach restaurant on Playa de San Cristóbal, the westernmost of Almuñécar's two main beaches. *Summer daily, otherwise daily except Tue | Paseo de las Flores | tel. 9 58 63 00 80 | Moderate*

TAPAS

The best places are around *Plaza de la Constitución (Town Hall Square), Plaza Kelibia* and behind *Paseo Puerta del Mar.*

BEACHES

The beaches extend from *Playa Velilla,* in the east, via *Puerta del Mar* and *Caletilla,* close to the town, to the long *Playa de San Cristóbal* in the west, where fishing boats are pulled up on the beach.

SPORTS & ACTIVITIES

Joggers keep fit along the promenades; between June and September an Aquapark is open on Playa Velilla *(www.aqua-tropic.com).*

ENTERTAINMENT

If you want to go out in the evening, head for the area between the Old Town and Playa Puerta del Mar, where there are several bars.

WHERE TO STAY

HELIOS

Its convenient location near the beach of San Cristóbal is just one advantage of this hotel block. Many � rooms have a sea view, pool. *232 rooms | Paseo de las Flores | tel. 9 58 63 06 36 | www.helios-hotels. com | Moderate*

MARCO POLO HIGHLIGHTS

VELILLA

Hostal near the eastern Velilla Beach, reasonable prices, all rooms with en-suite. *28 rooms | Paseo de Velilla 20 | tel. 958 63 07 58 | www.hostalvelilla.com | Budget*

INFORMATION

The *Palacete de la Najarra,* a small palace built in neo-Moorish style, provides the INSIDER TIP exotic setting for the Tourist Information Office. *Avenida de Europa | tel. 958 63 11 25 | www.turimoalmunecar.com*

WHERE TO GO

LA HERRADURA (127 E5) (*ω H5*)

Herradura means 'horseshoe', derived from the horseshoe-shaped bay on which this town of 3000 inhabitants is situated. Everything happens along the 2km (1mi) long beach, which is a good alternative to the beaches of Almuñécar, 8km (5mi) to the east. Behind the dark, stony beach is a hilly hinterland. Despite a few good restaurants such as *El Bambú (daily | Paseo Andrés Segovia | tel. 958 82 72 27 | Moderate),* La Herradura doesn't have the atmosphere and character of your typical 'multinational' tourist resort; it tends to be mostly Spanish families who come here.

MARINA DEL ESTE ●
(127 E5) (*ω H–J5*)

Marina del Este is one of the prettiest marinas in Andalusia, located approx. 5km (3mi) southwest of Almuñécar. Enclosed by steep hills and rocky promontories that drop abruptly into the sea, it is a peaceful little place, with a couple of outdoor restaurants in which to while away a pleasant lunchtime. Nearby is the *Playa Marina del Este,* a 150m/yds pebble beach.

INSIDER TIP PLAYA DE CANTARRIJÁN ☆☆ (127 D–E5) (*ω H5*)

This official nudist beach *(playa naturista),* approx. 12km (8 mi) west of Almuñécar, is stony and extends for about 300m/yds between two rocky headlands. A beach restaurant usually opens in the high season, otherwise visitors enjoy the seclusion and the scenic beauty of the cliffs, which are part of a small nature reserve, the *Paraje Natural Acantilados de Maro-Cerro Gordo.* The beach can be reached down a short (1.4km/1mi) road that turns off the ☆☆ N340 in the direction Nerja. It runs high above the coast and is well known for its fantastic views. The beach is also nice for non-nudists!

SALOBREÑA ★ (127 E5) (*ω J5*)

A dramatic crag topped by a castle and white sugar-cube houses tumbling down the hillside, Salobreña, 15km (9mi) east of Almuñécar, rises picturesquely from the coastal plain. Alleyways lead steeply to the upper village where the ☆☆ *Paseo de las Flores* viewing promenade surrounds the castle hill. There's usually a light breeze rustling through the palm trees and hedges of bougainvillea, and the view of the Sierra Nevada is stunning. A short distance outside the town, in the direction of Almuñécar, is the ☆☆ *Best Western Hotel Salobreña (198 rooms | N 340 km 323 | tel. 958 61 02 61 | www.bestwesternhotelsalobrena.com | Budget–Moderate).* What appears at first sight to be a rather charmless establishment actually provides INSIDER TIP excellent value for money as well as a very large pool. Those wanting something smaller and more exclusive might consider staying at the ☆☆ *Casa de los Bates (6 rooms | N 340 km 329.5 | tel. 958 34 94 95 | www.casadelosbates.com | Moderate),* a beautiful 19th-century country house perched on a hilltop, with fabulous gardens.

A Moorish castle dominates the old core of Salobreña, seaside resort for the Granadans

GRANADA

MAP INSIDE THE BACK COVER
(127 E3) (🗺 J4) **Granada, shortened to Graná in the Andalusian dialect,
is one of the most beautiful cities in Spain.
It is a place that lives and breathes history
at every turn; a city of students, plazas,
promenades, bars and intimate corners.**
Lying at the foot of the Sierra Nevada at
a height of around 700m (2300ft), the
provincial capital occupies a broad plateau, the Vega de Granada. In the 13th
century the Nasrid Dynasty made Granada the heart of their empire, a piece of
the orient in the occident, the last bas-
tion of the Moors on the Iberian Peninsula. The Catholic monarchs Ferdinand
and Isabella regained the city during the
Reconquista in 1492; Sultan Boabdil sur-
rendered his Alhambra, the 'Red Fortress',
without a struggle.
If you haven't seen Granada, you haven't
seen anything' goes a common local say-

ing. How true! The palace complex of the
Alhambra is like a spell from 'The Arabi-
an Nights', while the old Moorish quarter
of the Albaicín is a maze of countless alleyways and quaint corners. It is thanks
to these jewels that Granada (pop.
270,000) can be forgiven its unsightly

WHERE TO START?
The best place to soak up the
atmosphere of the city is around
Plaza Bib-Rambla (U C4) (🗺 c4).
You can then saunter through the
bustling Alcaicería; from there it's
not far to the Cathedral and the
Royal Chapel. The bus station is located quite a way out of the centre,
on Carretera de Jaén. From there,
buses Nos. 3 and 33 will take you
into the city. Car parks in the centre:
Puerta Real (Acera del Darro 30), El
Corte Inglés (Carrera del Genil) and
San Agustín (Plaza de San Agustín).

GRANADA

Monumental work of art with Sierra Nevada backdrop: the Alhambra

modern developments and traffic jams. Drivers should give the city a wide berth. In parts of the city, there's a video-monitored traffic ban for certain vehicles, something that isn't always obvious to outsiders. There's also a shortage of car parks and many of the hotels don't have their own parking. A civilised alternative to leaving your car in an expensive multi-storey car park is to park it just outside the city and take a taxi into the centre for a few euros. Once in the city, it's easy to get around on foot or by bus. If the climb up to the Albaicín or Sacromonte prove too tiring, simply hop aboard one of the public minibuses (nos. 31 and 34). To reach the Alhambra, walk up from Plaza Nueva via the Cuesta de Gomérez or take bus nos. 30 or 32. If you do decide to take the car, there is a large car park at the Alhambra, reached by following the well-signposted approach loop.

SIGHTSEEING

ALBAICÍN ★ (U D–E2) (ω d–e2)
Narrow alleyways criss-crossing the hillside; whitewashed houses with roof terraces and tiny patios; cypress trees, palm trees, plant pots, bougainvillea, overhead wires, colourful tiles on the walls, and the occasional patch of peeling paint or plaster: that is the Albaicín (also spelled Albayzín), once home to a substantial Muslim population. In the pedestrian street of *Calderería Nueva,* shady teashops *(teterías)* help to recreate the Moorish atmosphere. The quarter's alleyways climb steeply, culminating at the ● ☆ *Mirador de San Nicolás,* a vantage point with magnificent views of the Alhambra. Nearby, the mosque of *Mezquita Mayor* (garden and ☆ viewpoint accessible) reflects the fact that Muslims were not banished forever in 1492 – in fact, several thousand Muslims still call Granada their home. There is a second viewpoint, the ☆ *Mirador de San Cristóbal,* on the outer northern edge of the Albaicín, by the main road to Murcia.

ALHAMBRA ★ ●
(U D–E 3–4) (ω d–e 3–4)
Imposing from the outside, paradise on earth inside, the Alhambra or 'Red Fortress', named for the red clay of its formidable walls, was based on an ingenious concept. Constructed between the 13th

and 14th centuries for the rulers of the Nasrid dynasty, the central palace precinct was surrounded by massive, crenelated walls for protection and camouflage. This precinct, the *Palacios Nazaríes*, forms the heart the Alhambra, which is ranged across a plateau high above the ravine of the Darro River.

Apart from the palace precinct, the Alhambra includes three further areas: the *Alcazaba fortress*, the *Generalife* summer palace and the *Palacio de Carlos V* (see

separate entry), a Renaissance palace that was built on the Alhambra hill in the 16th century as a powerful symbol of the reconquista of Christianity over Islam. Bits of the Alhambra – thankfully relatively minor ones – were demolished to make way for its construction, as well as that of the neighbouring Church of Santa Maria. The Alcazaba housed the living quarters of the guards as well as silos and barns; it's possible to climb up the ⚜ *Torre de la Vela* for magnificent views over the city.

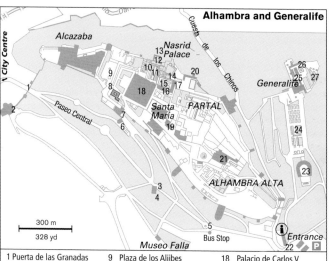

Alhambra and Generalife

1 Puerta de las Granadas
(Pomegranate Gate)
2 Torres Bermejas
(Red Towers)
3 Fuente del Tomate
(Tomato Fountain)
4 Monumento a Ganivet
(monument to writer
from Granada)
5 Fuente del Pimiento
(Paprika Fountain)
6 Pilar de Carlos V
(Column of Charles V)
7 Puerta de la Justicia
(Gate of Justice)
8 Puerto del Vino
(Wine Gate)

9 Plaza de los Aljibes
(Cistern Court)
10 Mexuar (former audience
chamber)
11 Patio de los Arrayanes
(Myrtle Court)
12 Salón de Embajadores
(Ambassadors' Hall)
13 Torre de Comares
14 Sala de las Dos Hermanas
(Hall of Two Sisters)
15 Patio de los Leones
(Lion Court)
16 Sala de los Abencerrajes
(Hall of the Abencerrajes)
17 Sala de los Reyes
(Hall of the Kings)

18 Palacio de Carlos V
(Palace of Charles V)
19 Baños (baths)
20 Torre de las Damas
21 Parador de San Francisco
22 Entrance to Alhambra
and Generalife
23 Theatre
24 Jardines nuevos
(New Gardens)
25 Patio de la Acequia
(Pool Court)
26 Patio de la Sultana
(Court of the Sultana)
27 Jardines altos
(Upper Gardens)

Ornate strapwork, intricately carved stucco, horseshoe arches, forests of columns, arabesques and calligraphy (pictorial representations are forbidden by Islam), stalactite ceiling decorations and repeated rhombus patterns are just some of the typical Moorish features you will encounter during a tour of the Palacios Nazaríes. The entrance to the precinct leads through the comparatively plain-looking palace reception hall, the *Mexuar,* which was converted into a chapel by Catholic monarchs, to the first richly decorated courtyard, the *Patio del Cuarto Dorado.* From here, a passageway leads through to the Court of the Myrtles, the *Patio de los Arrayanes,* where myrtle hedges frame a long pond in which the walls of the adjacent Torre de Comares are calmly reflected, creating one of the Alhambra's most enchanting vistas. The tower houses the Ambassadors' Hall, the *Salón de Embajadores,* where the Nasrid rulers received foreign diplomats. Spanned by a canopy consisting of 8017 individual pieces of cedar wood, it is the largest hall in the Alhambra.

A passage leads from the Court of Myrtles to the exquisite Court of the Lions, the *Patio de los Leones,* the basin of its central fountain supported by 12 marble lions. The filigree arcade surrounding the patio incorporates 124 marble columns. This courtyard provides access to the *Sala de los Abencerrajes* and the *Sala de las Dos Hermanas*, both of which have ceilings of the most amazing stalactite stuccowork. It was also the way in to the harem. All the rooms were heated by charcoal braziers, while the mashrabiyyah shutters enabled people to see out without being seen themselves.

Pools and gardens are integral to the palace complex, and beautiful views open out over the Albaicín. The *Generalife,* the Nasrids' summer palace, is situated above the Alhambra. It features labyrinthine gardens with water features and topiaries, radiating from the *Patio de la Acequia.* In the gardens, winding paths alternate with broad promenades, the trickling fountains and water channels exuding a restful effect.

A visit to the Alhambra needs planning in advance, especially during the high summer season. While you can buy same-day tickets directly from the Alhambra ticket office, there's only a limited number available, so you would need to start queuing very early in the morning to be sure of securing some. Booking in ad-

LOW BUDGET

▶ At Granada's municipal tourist offices on Plaza del Carmen and in the *Parque de las Ciencias (Tue–Sat 10am–7pm, Sun 10am–3pm | Avenida de la Ciencia)* the city ticket *Bono Turístico de Granada* is available for a reduced price: it costs 25 euros for three days and 30 euros for five days; among other attractions it includes entry to the Alhambra and Cathedral, as well as five or nine free rides on public buses respectively. At the central branch of the Caja Granada on Plaza Isabel la Católica the ticket costs 2 or 2.50 euros more. There is also a version for children, called the *Bono Infantil.*

▶ Admission to the lower level of Palacio de Carlos V in Granada is free. It houses the ● *Museo de la Alhambra (Tue–Sun 9am–2pm),* with displays of Hispano-Moorish art from the Middle Ages with ceramics, stucco and inlay work.

vance is strongly recommended; this can be done by credit card through the website *www.alhambra-tickets.es* or by calling *tel. 0034 934923750 (English, French, Spanish; leave off the country code if calling from within Spain).* A maximum of 10 tickets (each costing 14.30 euros) per person can be ordered. The visiting times are specified and no excep-

former sauna and relaxation rooms with their well-preserved brick walls and vaults, horseshoe arches and star-shaped skylights. *Tue–Sat 10am–2pm | Carrera del Darro 31*

CAPILLA REAL ★ ● (U C3) (𝄞 c3)

The late Gothic splendour of the Royal Chapel attached to the Cathedral is the

An oasis of tranquillity, a cool, green idyll: Patio de la Acequia in the Generalife Gardens

tions are made for latecomers! One interesting option is the late-evening visit *(visita nocturna). March–Oct daily 8.30am–8pm, Tue–Sat also 10–11.30pm, Nov–Feb daily 8.30am–6pm, Fri/Sat also 8–9.30pm | www.alhambra-patronato.es*

BAÑOS ÁRABES (EL BAÑUELO) (U D3) (𝄞 d3)

An inconspicuous entrance leads to the 11th-century Arab baths. In medieval times Granada had 21 of these thermal baths, and for the Moors they weren't just for washing but also for resting the mind and body as well as socialising. A small courtyard provides access to the

setting for the tomb of Spain's most important royals: Isabella of Castille (1451–1504) and Ferdinand of Aragón (1452–1516), the 'Catholic Monarchs'. Under their rule, during which Moorish Granada fell and Columbus discovered America, a new era was ushered in, not just for Spain but for the whole of Europe. The Italian Domenico Fancelli created the tomb, which is adorned with marble effigies of the royal couple. The chapel is also the last resting place of their heir to the Castilian throne, Joanna the Mad (1479–1555) and her husband Philip the Handsome (1478–1506), as well as one of Ferdinand and Isabella's grandchil-

dren. Steps lead down into the simple crypt containing the five lead coffins. The showpieces in the adjacent museum are Ferdinand's sword and Isabella's crown and sceptre. *April–Oct Mon–Sat 10.30am–1pm and 4–7pm, Sun 11am–1pm and 4–7pm, Nov–March Mon–Sat 10.30am–1pm and 3.30–6.30pm, Sun 11am–1pm and 3.30–6.30pm | Calle Oficios 3 | www.capillarealgranada.com*

CASA DE LOS PISA (U D3) (*𝄜 d3*)

The Casa de los Pisa is an especially beautiful and well-preserved Renaissance palace, notable for its **INSIDERTIP** fine courtyard. The palace contains a museum dedicated to the memory of San Juan de Dios (1495–1550). The saint spent the last part of his life in Granada, where he devoted himself to serving the poor and needy, founding a charity hospital and caring for the sick and the lame. He became a friend of the Pisa family and died in this house. You can see his deathbed on the guided tour; the saint lies buried in the Baroque basilica that is dedicated to him. *Mon–Sat 10am–1.30pm | Calle Convalecencia 1 | www.museosanjuandedios.es*

CASA DE LOS TIROS (U C–D4) (*𝄜 c–d4*)

This Spanish Renaissance-style fortified palace dates from the 16th century and now houses a museum of regional culture. Among the exhibits are ceramics, royal portraits, historic views of the Alhambra and paintings with folk themes. The Golden Room (*Cuadra Dorada*) is adorned with a lavishly decorated ceiling. *Tue 2.30–8.30pm, Wed–Sat 9am–8.30pm, Sun 9am–2.30pm | Calle Pavaneras 19 | www.museosdeandalucia.es*

INSIDERTIP CASA-MUSEO FEDERICO GARCÍA LORCA (HUERTA DE SAN VICENTE) (U A5) (*𝄜 a5*)

Once well outside the city, this estate is now on its outskirts and within earshot of the traffic on the ring road. The chalk-

A mausoleum built for the 'Catholic Monarchs' Ferdinand und Isabella: the Capilla Real

white property served as the summer home of Federico García Lorca and his family from 1926 to 1936; here Andalusia's greatest dramatist found the time and space to create new works. The guided tour takes about 30 minutes and leads into the lounge, kitchen and the piano room, which is graced by a painting by Lorca's friend, Salvador Dalí. Upstairs, Federico's room contains his bed and desk, and the neighbouring rooms are used for temporary exhibitions dedicated to the poet's life and work. The Huerta de San Vicente is surrounded by the beautifully laid out Parque García Lorca. On Wednesdays, admission to the museum is free! *April–June and Sept Tue–Sun 10am–12.30pm and 5–7.30pm, July/Aug 10am–2.30pm, Oct–March 10am–12.30pm and 4–6.30pm | Calle Virgen Blanca | www.huertadesanvicente.com*

INSIDER TIP CASA-MUSEO MANUEL DE FALLA (U E4) *(ɲ e4)*

Manuel de Falla (1876–1946) is one of Spain's greatest composers. Between 1922 and 1939, the year he migrated to Argentina, he lived in this *carmen*, a typical Granada-style whitewashed villa with blue shutters. Here, high above the rooftops of the city, he enjoyed 'the most beautiful view on earth', as he described it. He entertained many famous artist friends in the salon. The painter Ignacio Zuloaga liked to come here, as did Federico García Lorca and the later Nobel prize-winning poet Juan Ramón Jiménez. A guided tour of the house takes in the kitchen, the composer's studio with its piano, and the bedrooms of Falla and his sister. A lot of Falla's belongings have been preserved, including his collection of ties and hats. *Tue–Sat, July/Aug Thu–Sun, 10am–2pm | Calle Antequeruela Alta 11 | www.museomanueldefalla.com*

CATEDRAL (U C3) *(ɲ c3)*

More than 100m/yds long, Granada's cathedral is known for its vast proportions. First begun in 1518 by Enrique Egas, then continued from about 1530 in Renaissance style by Diego de Siloé, its construction carried on until 1704. Alonso Cano's Baroque facade was one of the last elements to be incorporated, but even then the tower remained incomplete. Inside the cavernous interior it is easy to feel lost amid the enormous columns, organ pipes and Cano's huge canvases. Alonso Cano (1601–1667) was a painter and sculptor as well as an architect. *Mon–Sat 10.45am–1.30pm and 4–7pm, Sun 4–7pm, April–Oct to 8pm | Gran Vía de Colón*

MONASTERIO DE LA CARTUJA (O) *(ɲ O)*

Founded in 1506, this Carthusian monastery is situated a little outside central Granada, but it is well worth a visit for the exuberant Baroque decoration of the church and sacristy. *April–Oct, daily 10am–1pm and 4–8pm, Nov–March 10am–1pm and 3–6pm | Paseo de la Cartuja*

MONASTERIO DE SAN JERÓNIMO (U B2–3) *(ɲ b2–3)*

After the fall of Muslim Granada and with the support of the Christian monarchy, it didn't take long for the religious orders to establish themselves in the city. They included the Hieronymites, who were responsible for this monastic complex built in 1504–1563. Today it is home to a tiny community of the female branch of the order. Highlights of a visit are the two-storey cloisters with orange trees and a nice view of the bell tower, and the vaulted interior where the main chapel has a magnificent altarpiece with INSIDER TIP colourful and ornate reliefs and sculptures. *April–Oct daily 10am–2pm and*

4–7.30pm, Nov–March 10am–1.30pm and 3–6.30pm | Compás de San Jerónimo

MUSEO ARQUEOLÓGICO Y ETNOLÓGICO (U D3) *(ℳ d3)*

The setting alone of the archaeological and ethnological museum makes it well worth a visit. The 16th-century palace *Casa de Castril* has an interior courtyard with beautiful slender arches. The various rooms cover all epochs from the Stone Age to the Moorish era, both chronologically and thematically, with exhibits ranging from alabaster figurines to hand-axes and astrolabes to Roman gravestones. From the ↘↙ upper level of the interior courtyard there is a beautiful view of the Alhambra. Occasionally concerts are held in the courtyard. *Closed for renovation | Carrera del Darro 41 | www.museosde andalucia.es*

PALACIO DE CARLOS V (U E3) *(ℳ e3)*

With its square ground plan enclosing an open, round courtyard with a diameter of 30m (100ft), this palace is an unusual structure. Only two of the three storeys that were originally planned were completed. Named after Emperor Charles V, who was also King of Spain from 1516, the palace was never occupied and has never had a proper purpose. Today the lower level houses the *Alhambra Museum* (see 'Low Budget'); above it is the *Museum of Fine Art (Museo de Bellas Artes | March–Oct Tue 2.30–8pm, Wed–Sat 9am–8pm, Sun 9am–2.30pm, Nov–Feb Tue 2.30–6pm, Wed–Sat 9am–6pm, Sun 9am–2.30pm)*. In this regionally oriented museum, the spectrum ranges from the Renaissance to contemporary art. Among the highlights are the historic views of the Alhambra as well as works by local-born artists Alonso Cano (1601–1667) and Manuel Gómez Moreno (1870–1970). The arcaded courtyard is

freely accessible and nice and cool in the heat of summer.

PARQUE DE LAS CIENCIAS (O) *(ℳ O)*

You can find everything you need to know about this interactive science museum in the 'Travel with Kids' chapter.

PASEO DE LOS TRISTES ↘↙ (U E3) *(ℳ e3)*

At the end of the Carrera del Darro on the southern edge of the Albaicín, this promenade juts out above the Río Darro. Take a seat at a terrace restaurant or just relax on a bench to enjoy the stunning views of the Alhambra, which rises on the opposite bank of the river. It is particularly impressive at night when the 'Red Fortress' is illuminated in sublime splendour. INSIDER TIP ▸ A great spot for romantics.

PLAZA BIB-RAMBLA ● (U C4) *(ℳ c4)*

Thanks to its central situation and the busy alleyways, such as Calle Zacatín, that radiate from it, this is the meeting place in the Old Town. In the middle of the square a fountain featuring a statue of Neptune gurgles away, surrounded by cafés and restaurants. There are two more attractive squares in the vicinity: *Plaza de la Romanilla*, with the new Federico García Lorca cultural centre, has a good view of the cathedral tower, while around the shady *Plaza de la Trinidad* are several tapas bars that enjoy an excellent reputation among the Granadans.

PLAZA NUEVA (U C3) *(ℳ c3)*

An urban hub; the access point for the Albaicín and Alhambra; an atmospheric nightlife area – the Plaza Nueva is many different things. At the eastern end it merges with the *Plaza de Santa Ana*, which is dominated by the magnificent Renaissance facade of the former royal court, the *Real Chancillería*. Below Plaza

Santa Ana, the smallest of Granada's three rivers, the Río Darro, disappears into an underground channel. In Moorish times a mosque stood on the site of the present-day church of *Santa Ana*.

PLAZA DE LA UNIVERSIDAD
(U B3) (*b3*)

The noise level of the students is just as much a feature of this bustling square in front of the Law Faculty as the church of Santos Justo y Pastor. The square merges with the *Plaza de la Encarnación,* an ideal place to take a break in one of the cafés.

SACROMONTE ☆ (U F2) (*f2*)

Granada's picturesque district of Sacromonte is famous for its cave dwellings with their whitewashed entrances, its community of *gitanos*, 'gypsies' and, of course, its flamenco. It is said that the first *gitanos* came to Granada as metalworkers with the army of the Catholic Monarchs. Sacromonte lies at the very edge of the city, high above the Darro valley, with gardens, side views of the Alhambra, remains of the old city wall and a proliferation of agaves and prickly pears. Washing hangs in front of the houses, but not everywhere is well tended and obscure corners should be avoided at night. The route leads off Granada's beaten tourist tracks up to the INSIDER TIP *Museo Cuevas del Sacromonte (April–Oct daily 10am–2pm and 5–8.30pm, Nov–March 10am–2pm and 4–7pm | Barranco de los Negros | www.sacromontegranada.com).* This folklore museum showcases a series of adjacent caves and explains the cave dwellers' way of life. The sleeping quarters are always at the back of the cave, the kitchen area at the very front. There are also storage areas for tools and food, and cave stables for donkeys and mules. The visit can be rounded off with a nice drink on the terrace of the museum bar.

A short distance above the district, in the solitude of the mountains, lies the *Abadía del Sacromonte (Tue–Sun 11am–1pm and 4–6pm | Camino del Sacromonte),* an abbey dating from the 17th century. It has a small collection of art treasures as well as underground INSIDER TIP catacombs dating from the Roman period.

Granada's famous flamenco can be experienced in the district of Sacromonte

FOOD & DRINK

Granada is one of the best places in the region for tapas bars (see 'Entertainment').

ALACENA DE LAS MONJAS
(U C4) (*c4*)

Fine cuisine with well-prepared meat dishes and creative ideas, such as the starter aubergines with honey (*berenjenas a la miel). Closed Sun eve. | Plaza del Padre Suarez 5 | tel. 9 58 22 95 19 | www.alacenadelasmonjas.com | Expensive*

CARMEN DE SAN MIGUEL
(U D4) (🗺 d4)

Slightly hidden away beneath the Bermejas Towers of the Alhambra, this restaurant offers innovate Spanish cuisine. Good wine list and a lovely ☼ terrace with great views. *Closed Sunday, Sunday evening in winter | Plaza Torres Bermejas 3 | tel. 9 58 22 67 23 | www.carmensan miguel.com | Expensive*

NUEVO (U C4) (🗺 c4)

At the heart of a popular bar and restaurant area, the Nuevo has been going since 1963. There's a choice of several menus and *raciones*. You can sit inside under wooden beams or outside on the terrace. *Daily | Calle Navas 25 | tel. 9 58 22 67 63 | Budget–Moderate*

LAS TITAS (U D5) (🗺 d5)

Café-restaurant in a lovely pavilion with INSIDERTIP▶ relaxing terrace. Set in the park near the promenade on the Río Ge-nil, it is off the beaten track. Inexpensive lunch menu. *Daily | Paseo de la Bomba | tel. 9 58 12 00 19 | Budget–Moderate*

VIA COLÓN (U C3) (🗺 c3)

If you're looking for a spot with a terrace in the heart of the Old Town, this place next to the cathedral is perfect. The menu includes a wide choice of dishes, with specialities such as aubergines stuffed with monkfish and shrimp *(berenjenas rellenas)* and broad beans *(habas)* with Serrano ham and egg. *Daily | Gran Vía de Colón 13 | tel. 9 58 22 07 52 | www.restau ranteviacolon.es | Budget–Moderate*

SHOPPING

ALCAICERÍA (U C3–4) (🗺 c3–4)

Situated near the cathedral, the Alcaicería was the Moors' grand bazaar. The lanes of this Arab market are filled with hustle and bustle and sometimes it gets very crowded. The many small shops

FLAMENCO IN GRANADA

In this part of Andalusia, Granada is the best place to see flamenco. In the district of Sacromonte there are several hole-in-the-wall flamenco bars that put on shows. Under the vaulted ceilings of the cave venues, the castanets rattle to the sound of 'Ole', and the dancers stamp and tap on the wooden floors. It's a mixture of traditional flamenco and entertainment aimed at the tourists, but the quality of the performances is usually high. Some contributions, however, might come across as a little unemotional and tired, illustrating just how difficult it is to project flamenco in a commercial environment when it really has to come from the soul. Despite this, going to a show, which lasts 60 or 70 minutes, is a real experience. The entry price *(roughly 20–30 euros, booking strongly recommended in high season)* usually includes a drink. There are more expensive packages including dinner and transportation. Well-established venues include the *Cuevas Los Tarantos (Camino de Sacromonte 9 | tel. 9 58 22 45 25 | www.cuevaslostarantos. com)* and the *Cueva Venta El Gallo (Barranco de los Negros 5 | tel. 9 58 22 84 76 | www.ventaelgallo.com).* There are usually two shows, at 9.30 and 11pm.

are crammed with leather goods, trays, bags, scarves, costume jewellery, cushion covers and sacred figurines.

In the *Convento de San Bernardo (Calle Gloria 2* (U D3) *(🗺 d3))*, the little commu-

The alleyways of the Alcaicería have the atmosphere of a Moroccan souq

GUITAR MAKERS

There are several small, old-established firms, including, since 1875, the *Casa Ferrer,* which has a shop on the *Cuesta de Gomérez 26* (U D3) *(🗺 d3),* and the larger *Guitarrería Gil de Avalle (www.gildeavalle.com)* on *Plaza de Realejo 15* (U D4) *(🗺 d4).*

FASHION

There are several inexpensive clothes shops – as well as shoe shops – lining the *Calle Recogidas* (U A–B 4–5) *(🗺 a–b 4–5),* which starts at the Puerta Real. The *El Corte Inglés* department store on *Acera del Darro* (U C5) *(🗺 c5)* has everything under one roof. Smarter boutiques and shoe shops are concentrated in the core of the Old Town, in the pedestrian zone around *Calle Mesones* (U B4) *(🗺 b4)* and *Calle Zacatín* (U C4) *(🗺 c4).*

nity of Cistercian nuns sells an assortment of aniseed- and almond-flavoured confectionery, which they make themselves. The sisters at the *Monasterio de San Jerónimo (Compás de San Jerónimo* (U B2–3) *(🗺 b2–3))* produce home-made biscuits and lemon and orange marmalades, which you can purchase in their sales room. But none of it is that cheap!

DISCOTECA MAE WEST (U A5) *(🗺 a5)*
Popular megadisco in the Neptuno shopping centre. Lots of locals, various live acts. On Friday and Saturday it's packed to the rafters. *Calle Arabial | www.ibribones.com*

INSIDER TIP > SALA VIMAAMBI (U D3) *(🗺 d3)*
Small cultural centre with cinema and concerts. On Friday and Saturday evenings, at

9 and 10.30pm, their studio theatre stages the 'Raíz y Duende' flamenco show, with performances straight from the Albaicín, free of the 'folklore' that ruins some of the more tourist-oriented shows. For many of the young dance and music talents who perform here, it is a springboard into the professional limelight. *Cuesta de San Gregorio 30 | tel. 9 58 22 73 34 | www.vimaambi.com*

TAPAS BARS ★ ●

In Granada, the snacks still come free with your drink. Guide price: from 1.50 euros, for better wines a good 2.50–3euros for wine plus tapas. There are lots of stylish tapas bars clustered around *Plaza Nueva* (U C3) (*M c3*), particularly in *Calle de Elvira,* where you'll find such traditional establishments as the *Antigua Bodega Castañeda* and the *Taberna Salinas* (lots of students). Another nice area for tapas bars is *Calle Navas* (U C4) (*M c4*) near the city hall, where places like *La Chicotá, Las Copas* and the *Taberna Pata Negra* enjoy a good reputation among locals. An area less well known by outsiders but with several very pleasant haunts is the **INSIDER TIP** *Plaza Campo del Príncipe.*

ALHAMBRA PALACE HOTEL ☼
(U E4) (*M e4*)
Luxury hotel in an enormous neo-Moorish palace below the Alhambra plateau. Stunning views over the city. *126 rooms | Plaza Arquitecto García de Paredes 1 | tel. 9 58 22 14 68 | www.h-alhambrapalace. es | Expensive*

INSIDER TIP GAR-ANAT HOTEL DE PEREGRINOS (U C4) (*M c4*)
Small boutique hotel occupying a 17th-century mansion in the historic Jewish quarter of Realejo. The comfortable rooms lead off a courtyard, which has a 'Tree of Wishes', where you can hang a wish. Included in the price is the excellent breakfast buffet in the cellar, as well as nice little gestures such as biscuits in the afternoon and water bottles at night. Television is available on request.

Bodegas Castañeda has a large choice of delicious tapas

Choose a room at the back! *15 rooms | Placeta de los Peregrinos 1 | tel. 958 22 55 28 | www.hoteldeperegrinos. com | Moderate*

EL LADRÓN DE AGUA (U D3) (*d3*)
Small, friendly and atmospheric boutique hotel in a building dating from the 16th century on the edge of the Albaicín hill (not suitable for cars!). Various classes of room are available, all with a simple, refined elegance. As soon as you enter the covered courtyard with its wooden balustrades you feel welcome here. *15 rooms | Carrera del Darro 13 | tel. 958 215 040 | www.ladrondeagua.com | Moderate–Expensive*

LANDAZURI (U D3) (*d3*)
Reasonable prices and an excellent location between Plaza Nueva and the climb to the Alhambra make this pension an interesting proposition for low-budget travellers. Rooms with en-suite or shared bathrooms. *17 rooms | Cuesta de Gomérez 24 | tel. 958 22 14 06 | www.pension landazuri.com | Budget*

LA NINFA (U D4) (*d4*)
Hostal with decorated tile facade on one of the nicest squares in Granada. Friendly atmosphere and well looked after. Under the same ownership is the nearby *La Ninfa* restaurant (*Budget–Moderate*). *11 rooms | Plaza Campo drel Príncipe | tel. 958 22 79 85 | www.hostallaninfa.net | Budget*

OASIS BACKPACKERS' HOSTEL (U C3) (*c3*)
In a central location and a bargain for those who don't mind 6-, 8-, or 10-bedded rooms. Breakfast, internet, and tea and coffee are included in the price. With kitchen and roof terrace. *92 beds in 12 rooms | Placeta Correo Viejo 3 | tel.* *958 2158 48 | www.oasisgranada.com | Budget*

PARADOR DE SAN FRANCISCO (U E4) (*e4*)
This hotel is one of the most popular and expensive in the parador chain: in a perfect location on the Alhambra plateau, housed in a former Franciscan monastery. Book well in advance! *40 rooms | Real de la Alhambra | tel. 958 22 14 40 | www. parador.es | Expensive*

INFORMATION

Plaza del Carmen (U C4) (c4) | tel. 958 24 82 80 | www.turgranada.es; Plaza de Santa Ana (U D3) (d3) | tel. 958 57 52 02 | www.andalucia.org

WHERE TO GO

GUADIX (127 F3) (*K3–4*)
This town of 20,000 inhabitants, around 60km (40mi) east of Granada, is like nowhere else in Spain, for here several thousand people still live in underground cave dwellings. Around 2000 of these dwellings have been preserved. Some of the caves have their own open-air patios where the washing is hung out to dry, others can only be accessed down steps. In the picturesque ★ *Barrio de Cuevas* quarter, the *Cueva-Museo de Costumbres Populares* folk museum (*Mon–Fri 10am–2pm and 4–6pm, 5–7pm in summer, Sat 10am–2pm | www.cuevamuseoguadix. com*) provides an insight into underground living and architecture. It is interesting to learn that the cave dwellings have an average size of 70 sq m (750 sq ft), that the kitchen is always located at the front of the labyrinthine interiors, and that they have no windows – all natural light and ventilation come through the door.

GRANADA

From the cave quarter, a short path leads from *Plaza Padre Poveda* to ☀️ viewpoint *(mirador)*. This provides the best views of Guadix, taking in the Alcazaba (Moorish fortress), the cathedral tower and the bizarre-looking cliffs in the background. Around the viewpoint are the rooftops of the caves, as indicated by those distinctive white symbols of the town: the chimneys. Don't worry – the roofs won't fall in!

A further cave, the *Cueva La Alcazaba,* lies below the castle on Calle San Miguel. Occupying that particular underworld is the pottery museum, the *Museo de la Alfarería (Mon–Fri 10am–1pm and 4–7pm, 5–8pm in summer, Sat–Sun 10am–1.30pm | www.cuevamuseoalcazaba. com)* spread around several small rooms. In contrast to the modest caves, the Cathedral is full of religious pomp and splendour with a bombastic Baroque facade. Begun in 1492 over the ruins of a mosque, the edifice took more than 300 years to complete. The main emphasis of the cathedral museum *(Mon–Sat 10.30am–1pm and 4–6pm, in summer 5–7pm)* is on Baroque paintings and sculptures.

If the caves have aroused your curiosity, you can try staying in one of the **INSIDER TIP** cave hotels such as the *Cuevas Abuelo Ventura (13 rooms | Camino de Lugros 20 | tel. 9 58 66 40 50 | www.cuevas abueloventura.com | Budget).* Information: *Plaza de la Constitución | tel. 9 58 66 28 04 | www.guadixymarquesado.org*

SIERRA NEVADA ★ ●
(128 A–C 4–5) (∭ J–L4)

Rising majestically within sight of Granada, the Sierra Nevada *(sierranevada es)* is the roof of Andalusia and the highest mountain range on the Iberian Peninsula. It is crowned by ☀️ *Mulhacén* (3481m/11,421ft) and by ☀️ *Pico de Veleta* (3392m/11,129ft). In winter, the upper reaches are covered in snow and

FEDERICO GARCÍA LORCA

Federico García Lorca (1898–1936) was one of Spain's greatest poets and dramatists, and tragedies such as 'The House of Bernarda Alba' are still performed both at home and abroad. Born into affluent circumstances in the village of Fuente Vaqueros 18km (11mi) northwest of Granada, he always maintained a close bond with his home. His best-known book of poetry was 'Romancero Gitano' (Gypsy Ballads), published in 1928. In Huerta de San Vicente, his summer home in Granada, he wrote the theatre classics 'Yerma' and 'Blood Wedding'. He was a member of the influential group of poets called the *Gene-* *ración del 27* (Generation of '27) and among his closest companions was the Surrealist painter Salvador Dalí. Lorca's homosexuality and outspoken liberal views brought him enemies, and ultimately a tragic end: at the beginning of the Spanish Civil War in August 1936 he was captured and shot near Granada by right-wing rebels loyal to General Franco. In Fuente Vaqueros, his birthplace *(Casa Natal)* can be visited as part of a guided tour *(Tue–Sun 10am, 11am, 12pm, 1pm, Oct–March additionally Tue–Sat 4pm and 5pm, April–June and Sept 5pm and 6pm | Calle Poeta García Lorca 4 | www.patronatogarcialorca.org)*

On the summit of Pico de Veleta: on a clear day you can see Africa

ice, otherwise the range is characterised by jagged ridges of crag and scree. Most of the range is protected by the 860 sq km (330 sq mi) Parque Nacional de Sierra Nevada and extends into the Almería province. Geologically, this was once a heavily glaciated region, as can be seen from the U-shaped valleys and several dozen lakes. More than 2000 plant species have been documented, and with a bit of luck you should see golden eagles and ibex here.

The easiest way to reach the Sierra Nevada is to take the well-surfaced A395 mountain road, which winds its way up into the high mountains for about 35km (22mi) southeast of Granada. On the way you'll pass olive trees, then pine trees and small gorges where nets are in place to protect against rockfall. The higher you go, the bigger the mountain panorama, until you get to *Pradollano,* the Sierra' Nevada's ski resort at an altitude of 100m (6890ft), with attendant shops, ski-schools, restaurants, cafés, bars and nightclubs. Outside the ski season it all looks a bit forlorn. You can continue your journey along the A395 beyond Pradollano, until it stops at the 2500m sign and a car park. From there, hikers set off into the high mountains.

Towards the south, the Sierra Nevada drops to the foothills of the Alpujarra, a scenic area scattered with pretty villages. Here, too, a road from the south approaches the mountains via Lanjarón und Capileira, but the ascent is closed to private vehicles for reasons of environmental protection. Instead, between the months of May and October – and depending on the weather and latest regulations – a shuttle bus takes visitors from Capileira at 1420m (4659ft) to the 2700-m (8858-ft) high a Mirador de Trevélez, which provides access to some magnificent hiking country. Information is available from the *Punto de Información (tel. 9 58 76 30 90)* in Capileira. A journey through the glorious landscape of the Alpujarra is described in the 'Trips & Tours' chapter.

COSTA DEL SOL
AROUND MÁLAGA

In terms of resorts, the eastern and central Sun Coast encompass everything from the heavily built up and brash to the more modest and laid-back. Popular bases include Torremolinos and Nerja, while the marina of Benalmádena is one of the nicest in Spain. Right in the middle of the coast is the engaging city of Málaga, the birthplace of Pablo Picasso. The coastal strip rises to totally unspoiled landscapes, complete with olive groves, vineyards and white villages.

As far as the beaches are concerned, the picture is mixed: there are small ones, sometimes divided into several bays as at Nerja, and long continuous beaches such as the one in Torremolinos. But there are no secret, hidden-away places any more; in summer all the beaches are packed.

MÁLAGA

MAP INSIDE THE BACK COVER
(126 B–C5) (*Ø G5*) 'In Málaga you feel like you've been carried off to Africa: the dazzling white of the houses, the deep indigo blue of the sea, the murderous glare – all contribute to this illusion' wrote the French poet Théophile Gautier in the mid-19th century. The illusion has long since disappeared. The provincial capital of Málaga (pop. 570,000) is anything but love at first or even second sight – but if you get to know it, affection grows. Behind the rings of high-rises, the port facilities and the constant drone of traffic, there is enduring evidence of a long and eventful past, a

Photo: Málaga

Málaga in the centre of the Costa del Sol is the main gateway to the region. It's a springboard for the highlife of the coast and the high hills of the interior

WHERE TO START?

The best point of reference in Málaga is **Plaza de la Merced (131 E1–2)** (*III I1–2*), the location of Picasso's birthplace. Bus and rail travellers arrive a little way out of the centre at the station on Paseo de los Tilos, from where it's roughly a 15-minute walk to the city. Car parks near the centre include Plaza de la Marina and Plaza de la Merced.

well as some stunning vistas: the Cathedral and Old Town, the pedestrian zone, two Moorish fortresses and a multi-faceted museum culture, led by the Picasso Museum. Founded by the Phoenicians as Malaka, today the city is a popular cruise port. The city fathers have ambitious plans for further development, some of which have been partly realised. They range from harbour renovations at Paseo de los Curas to new museums and even the construction of a metro with two lines (*www.metrodemalaga.info*).

MÁLAGA

SIGHTSEEING

ALCAZABA ⚘ (131 E2) (*l2*)

Built on a hill rising above the Old Town, the Alcazaba was the stronghold of Moorish governors from the 11th century.

CASTILLO DE GIBRALFARO ★ ⚘ (131 F2) (*m2*)

Connected to the Alcazaba by a double defensive wall, the Moors' upper castle dates from the 14th century. It functioned as a lookout post over the city and also

Málaga's cathedral 'La Manquita' was never completed despite taking 250 years to build

It is the best preserved fortress palace in Spain, with typical Moorish features such as horseshoe arches still intact. While some of the restoration is over the top, and hibiscus bushes, bougainvillea and pools have softened the military severity of the complex, it's worth climbing up for the views over the port, with its cranes and ships, the pleasant Paseo del Parque, and the Cathedral. The vista also takes in the bullring. A good-value combination ticket is available for the Alcazaba and the Castillo de Gibralfaro. *Summer Tue–Sun 9.30am–8pm, otherwise 8.30am–7pm| Calle de la Alcazabilla*

boasted considerable firepower. Today the fort is a peaceful island of greenery where you can stroll along the much restored crenellated battlements and enjoy great views over the tops of pine trees to the city, coast and hinterland. It is amazing how abruptly Málaga stops; orientation panels help with the geography. In the central courtyard there's a small museum. *Summer daily 9am–8pm, otherwise 9am–6pm*

CATEDRAL DE LA ENCARNACIÓN (131 D2) (*j2*)

Málaga's cathedral exudes strength and power. Built on the site of a forme

mosque, its construction spanned more than 200 years (1528–1782), although it was never actually completed. It is known locally as La Manquita, 'the one-armed one', because only one of the two towers that were planned was built. In the cavernous interior, gigantic columns rise to the 40-m (130-ft) high vaults.

The dimensions, the distance between the altar and the pews, as well as the lavish decor and oil paintings in the various chapels don't exactly make for a contemplative atmosphere. But the choir stalls, by Pedro de Mena, are a sculptural masterpiece. Typical of Spain, the organ has horizontal pipes in order to improve the acoustics and to prevent dust getting in.

In the chapel of the Virgen de los Reyes, there is a dramatic painting of the 'Be-heading of St Paul'. The cathedral's eponym is to be found in the chapel of Nuestra Señora de la Encarnación. Also well worth seeing are the sculptures and oil paintings of saints in the small cathedral museum, including a portrait of St Paul by José de Ribera. *Mon–Fri 10am–6pm, Sat 10am–5pm | Calle Molina Lario*

CENTRO DE ARTE CONTEMPORÁNEO (CAC) ● (130 B4) (ω h4)

Housed in the former Rationalist-style wholesale market, this is a great venue for contemporary art, with lovely big display spaces. There are no permanent exhibitions, but it stages good temporary shows that rely in part on the centre's own collection. Big names such as Louise Bourgeois, Rebecca Horn, Andy Warhol, Olafur Eliasson, Anselm Kiefer and Richard Serra have all been exhibited here. Free admission. *Summer Tue–Sun 10am–2pm and 5–9pm, otherwise Tue–Sun 10am–8pm | Calle Alemania | cacmalaga.org*

MUSEO AUTOMOVILÍSTICO MÁLAGA (0) (ω 0)

Incorporating part of the old tobacco factory, this fascinating museum contains beautiful vintage motorcars from all over the world. It takes you on a journey through time, as the aesthetic and technical development of the motorcar is re-

⭐ **Castillo de Gibralfaro in Málaga**
High above the city stands the old Moorish castle – enjoy the views from the ramparts
→ p. 66

⭐ **Museo Picasso in Málaga**
Immerse yourself in the worlds of Picasso in his hometown of Málaga – a real experience!
→ p. 68

⭐ **Antequera**
Special features of the town are its megalithic burial mounds (dolmen) with their long tunnel entrances and massive stone supports → p. 71

⭐ **Balcón de Europa in Nerja**
This promenade above the sea is the town's main meeting place → p. 73

⭐ **Cueva de Nerja**
A wonder of nature, these caves are worth visiting despite being so busy → p. 74

⭐ **Frigiliana**
Alleyways weave their way between pretty, whitewashed houses – out and about in Frigiliana → p. 76

vealed. *Tue–Sun 10am–7pm | Avenida Sor Teresa Prat 15 | www.museoautomovil malaga.com*

MUSEO CARMEN THYSSEN
(130 C2) *(⌀ j2)*

A mix of old and modern architecture provides the setting for this notable art museum, which is based on the collection of Baroness Carmen Thyssen-Bornemisza. Born in Barcelona in 1943, she became a model, wife of the American actor Lex Barker, who played Tarzan, and later of the billionaire art collector Hans-Heinrich Thyssen-Bornemisza. The exhibits in the permanent collection include a 'Santa Marina' by the master Francisco de Zurbarán (1598–1664) and works by Spanish painters from the 19th and 20th centuries, including Guillermo Gómez Gil, Joaquín Sorolla and Julio Romero de Torres, who concentrated on more everyday scenes and themes. There are also temporary exhibitions (combined ticket). *Tue–Thu and Sun 10am–8pm, Fri/Sat 10am–9pm, July/Aug Mon–Sat 10am–8pm| Calle Compañía 10 | www.carmen thyssenmalaga.org*

MUSEO DE LA COFRADÍA DE LOS ESTUDIANTES (131 E2) *(⌀ l2)*

Málaga's 3000-strong student fraternities play a big part in the city's Easter processions, when gigantic floats *(tronos)* are carried through the streets, their smallest details shining in gold and silver. This museum reveals many of the secrets of this very Spanish tradition. *Mon–Fri 10am–1pm | Calle de la Alcazabilla 3*

INSIDER TIP MUSEO INTERACTIVO DE LA MÚSICA (131 D3) *(⌀ j3)*

The location of this well-devised interactive music museum, hidden under the Plaza de la Marina by the entrance to an underground car park, is every bit as surprising as its contents. Several hundred instruments take visitors on a journey through the musical traditions of many different countries and periods. In the ethnographic section you'll encounter instruments made of bone and shells; elsewhere you'll find instruments that can be touched and played, so you can drum, pluck and blow to your heart's content. *Mon–Fri 10am–2pm and 4–8pm, Sat/Sun 11am–3pm and 4.30–8.30pm | www.musicaenaccion.com*

MUSEO PICASSO ★ ● (131 E2) *(⌀ l2)*

It was the wish of Pablo Picasso (1881–1973) that a representative collection of his work be displayed in the city of his birth (Picasso's family lived in Málaga until 1891) – and that makes Málaga a prime address when it comes to art. In the Renaissance Buenavista Palace the world of the great artist, master of a variety of styles, techniques and materials, is revealed – with early and late works, oil paintings, sketches and ceramics all on show. Pictures of bulls betray his Spanish soul, portraits of women his passions. Exhibits in the permanent collection include, among others: *Búho sobre una silla* ('Owl Sitting on a Chair'), *Jacqueline sentada* ('Seated Jacqueline') and *Naturaleza muerta con cráneo y tres erizos* ('Still Life with Skull and Three Hedgehogs'). The works, which range from his earliest to last creative phase, are priceless, and each room is a little artistic adventure in itself. The INSIDER TIP museum café is the perfect place to take a break, and the basement of the former palace holds a surprise that has nothing at all to do with Picasso: Roman and Phoenician remains, some of them over 2500 years old. On the website there's a link for advance booking. There's also a space for temporary exhibitions (special ticket or combined entry

with the permanent collection). *Tue–Thu and Sun 10am–8pm, Fri/Sat 10am–9pm | Calle de San Agustín 8 | www.museo picassomalaga.org*

PLAZA DE LA MERCED
(131 E1–2) ( *l1–2*)

An obelisk in the centre, lots of pigeons, benches and cafés – impressions of one of Málaga's main squares, which is also

been in operation until the 3rd century. In the Middle Ages, the Moors used the site as a quarry for building the Alcazaba, and it was only in the mid-20th century, during excavation work for a park, that the remains were rediscovered. The stands have been substantially restored. *Sun 10am–2.30pm, Tue–Sat April–Oct 10am–9pm, Nov–March 9am–7pm | Calle de la Alcazabilla*

Plaza de la Merced, where a bronze statue of Picasso stands in front of his birthplace

the location of Pablo Picasso's birthplace. The Picasso Foundation runs the *Museo Casa Natal (daily 9.30am–8pm | funda cionpicasso.malaga.eu)*, a modest museum in which photos recall the little Pablo, and temporary exhibitions the great Picasso.

TEATRO ROMANO (131 E2) ( *l2*)

The remains of this Roman theatre are at the entrance to the Alcazaba. It dates from the 1st century AD and would have

FOOD & DRINK

BODEGUITA DE CARLOS
(130 C2) ( *j2*)

Typical Málagan restaurant serving fish and other seafood, in the heart of the historic district. *Daily, Fernando de Lesseps | tel. 9 52 22 21 63 | Budget*

CAFÉ DE PARÍS (131 F3) ( *m3*)

A prime example of the sophisticated modern cuisine of Andalusia, headed by

Jose Carlos Garcia. The dishes are seasonal, based on fresh ingredients from the market, and therefore always changing. *Closed Sun/Mon | Plaza de la Capilla/ Muelle 1 | tel. 9 52 00 35 88 | www. rcafedeparis.com | Expensive*

EL JARDÍN (131 D2) (*ſŪ k2*)

This traditional eatery next to the cathedral is a mix of café and restaurant. There are simple dishes and salads, but also more sophisticated food, such as braised oxtail or marinated partridge. *Closed Sun | Calle Cañón 1 | tel. 9 52 22 04 19 | Budget–Moderate*

MONTANA (O) (*ſŪ O*)

Modern Mediterranean cuisine, including some very elaborate creations, in the stylish setting of a late 19th-century palace. There's a choice of two taster menus. *Closed Mon | Calle Compás de la Victoria 5 | tel. 9 52 65 12 44 | www.restaurante montana.es | Expensive*

SHOPPING

There's a great selection of boutiques and shoe shops in the area around *Calle Puerta del Mar, Calle Nueva* and *Calle Marqués de Larios* (130–131 C–D 2–3) (*ſŪ j–k 2–3*). There's also plenty of choice in shopping centres such as the *Málaga Plaza (Calle Armengual de la Mota 12* (130 B2) (*ſŪ h2*) *| www.malaga plaza.com)* and *Larios Centro (Avenida de la Aurora 25* (130 A3) (*ſŪ g3*) *| www. larioscentro.com).*

BEACHES

Málaga, a city of half a million people with a busy industrial area, is hardly going to be the ideal seaside holiday destination. The 14km (9mi) of rather unattractive city beaches, some of them with

a view of the port, begin east of the harbour basin with the *Playa de la Malagueta* and continue as far as the marina of *El Candado*.

ENTERTAINMENT

You can find tapas bars in the centre near Plaza de la Constitución around *Pasaje de Chinitas* and *Calle Moreno Monroy.* Opera and ballet is performed at the *Teatro Cervantes (Calle Ramos Marín* (131 E1) (*ſŪ l1*) *| tel. 9 52 22 41 00 | www.teatrocervantes. com).* There are pop concerts and DJs at the *Wakame (Calle Correo Viejo 4* (131 D2) (*ſŪ k 2)*) and *Intercambio Málaga (Calle Huerto del Conde 7* (131 E1) (*ſŪ l1)*), among other venues. For flamenco featuring performances by promising young talent, visit the *Liceo Flamenco* at *Calle Beatas 21 (*(131 D1–2) (*ſŪ k1–2*) *| www.li ceoflamenco.com).* You'll find an up-to-date weekly programme of Málaga events at *www.youthingmalaga.com.*

WHERE TO STAY

DON PACO (130 A5) (*ſŪ g5*)

Comfortable hotel in a busy area near the railway and bus stations. *31 rooms | Calle Salitre 53 | tel. 9 52 31 90 08 | www. hotel-donpaco.com | Budget*

NH MÁLAGA (130 B3) (*ſŪ h3*)

Comfortable 4-star hotel, located near the city next to a bridge across the dry riverbed of the Rio Guadalmedina. It's part of the NH chain. Big price fluctuations, INSIDER TIP▸ good breakfast buffet. *133 rooms | Calle San Jacinto 2 | tel. 9 52 07 13 23 | www.nh-hoteles.es | Moderate–Expensive*

PETIT PALACE PLAZA (131 D2) (*ſŪ k2*)

Located in the heart of the city, with thoughtful touches; each room has a

computer. *66 rooms | Calle Nicasio 3 | tel. 9 52 22 21 32 | www.hthoteles.com | Moderate*

INFORMATION

Plaza de la Marina 11 (131 D3) (*@ k3*) *tel. 9 51 92 60 20 | www.malagaturismo.com*

WHERE TO GO

ANTEQUERA ⭐ (126 B4) (*@ F4*)

Dolmens and churches, a nice Old Town and a Moorish castle – these are reasons enough for a detour to Antequera (pop. 30,000), which lies 50km (30mi) to the north. But don't go on Monday, when the most important attractions are closed. A trip to Antequera can easily be combined with a visit to Lobo Park or a walk in the nature reserve of *El Torcal de Antequera* (see 'Excursions and Tours' chapter). But to do all this in just a day from the coast would be quite demanding.

It may therefore be a good idea to stay in Antequera, where accommodation options include the *Parador (58 rooms | Paseo García del Olmo 2 | tel. 9 52 84 02 61 | www.parador.es | Moderate)* and the centrally located *Hotel Coso Viejo (42 rooms |*

Calle Encarnación 9 | tel. 9 52 70 50 45 | www.hotelcosoviejo.es | Budget), which occupies an 18th-century townhouse. You can eat well at both hotels. Information: *Plaza de San Sebastián 7 | tel. 9 52 70 25 05 | turismo.antequera.es*

Among Antequera's most impressive attractions are its burial mounds, or dolmen. These megalithic graves are between 4000 and 5000 years old and are the largest such structures in Europe. The *Menga* and *Viera* dolmen are part of an archaeological complex on the way into town from Málaga, while *El Romeral* stands on its own, to the northeast of the town centre *(opening times for all three dolmen Tue–Sat 9am–6pm, Sun 9.30am–2.30pm).* Tunnels lead into Viera and El Romeral, while inside Menga there is a large, atmospherically lit chamber with enormous roof slabs and supports.

In the historic district of *Coso Viejo,* you can stroll across Plaza de San Sebastián, which has a church of the same name, its tower crowned by a weathervane with the figure of an angel (El Angelote), and Plaza Coso Viejo, where there is an equestrian statue of King Ferdinand I, who wrested Antequera from the Moors in 1410. Dominating the hill above the Old

The Viera dolmen in Antequera: this megalithic burial chamber was discovered in the 20th century

Town is the beautifully restored Moorish castle, the ☀ *Alcazaba (summer Tue–Sun 10.30am–2pm and 6–8.30pm, winter very changeable but always a lot shorter).* From there, you'll get the best view over Antequera's white sea of houses, of the surrounding olive groves, the Sierra de Chimenea and the enormous isolated crag of limestone called La Peña de los Enamorados, or 'The Lovers' Leap', which juts out of the plain like a giant fin. On the plateau, there is also the Renaissance church *Real Colegiata de Santa María.*

On the way to or back from Antequera, take the route that passes through the mountain town of Álora to take a detour to the *Paraje Natural Desfiladero de los Gaitanes,* where the Guadalhorce river has sliced through limestone to create a spectacular gorge, the Desfiladero de los Gaitanes, otherwise known as 'El Chorro'. To the west of the gorge, a lonely high-level road leads to the ruins of the settlement of Bobastro dating from the 9th/10th century and up to ☀ viewpoint *(mirador)* with beautiful views over the nearby reservoirs of Embalse de Guadalhorce and Embalse Tajo de la Encantada and the barren mountain wilderness in which they lie. Bear in mind, however, that the road signs in the area are not very good.

JARDÍN BOTÁNICO-HISTÓRICO LA CONCEPCIÓN (126 B5) (*ⓜ F5*)

Araucaria, rubber trees, magnolias and giant bamboo are rooted in this 'historical-botanical garden', which was originally created in the mid-19th century by the Marquis and Marchioness of Loring, in the hills just 10km (7mi) north of Malaga. Walking around, you'll encounter a rich collection of flora and fauna from all continents; coolness is provided by little waterfalls and streams. There are various different routes you can take depending on the time you have available – 'Jewels of Concepción', 'Themed Gardens', 'Around the World in 80 Trees' and the 'Forest Route'. The gardens are signposted off the Antequera motorway. *Tue–Sun 9.30am–8.30pm, Oct–March until 5.30pm | laconcepcion.malaga.eu*

INSIDER TIP LOBO PARK ☺ (126 B4) (*ⓜ F5*)

Their graceful movement, their lonely, penetrating eyes, their clear hierarchy in the pack – wolves! You will encounter some 25 of these magnificent creatures in this wolf park to the southwest of Antequera (60km/37mi northwest of Málaga, approach via Álora or Antequera). The enclosures cover a total area of 10 hectares (25 acres) and are dotted with shrubs and stone oaks. There are timber wolves from Canada, as well as Alaskan, Iberian and European wolves. Daniel and Alexandra, the German couple who own the park, give the animals as much space as possible in which to play, hunt and relax. The visit takes the form of a 90-minute guided tour. Paths around the enclosures and individual platforms allow visitors to observe the wolves' natural behaviour. Most of the wolves were born in the park and are used to having people around them. There is also a petting farm with pigs, sheep and goats. From May to October (and on nights of the full moon in winter) you can experience a Wolf Howl Night; for reservations *tel. 9 52 03 11 07. Daily 10am–6pm, tours usually Mon–Fri 11am, 1pm, 3pm and 4.30pm, Sat/Sun 11am, 12pm, 1pm, 2pm, 3pm and 4.30pm | Carretera A 343 Antequera–Álora km 16 | www.lobopark.com*

MONTES DE MÁLAGA (126 B–C5) (*ⓜ G5*)

This mountainous region just north of Málaga is swathed in dense forest, dominated by the Aleppo pines that were plant-

Nerja: unspoiled charm, not least thanks to the lack of hotel blocks

ed here in the 1930s in a major programme of reforestation. The hills themselves reach heights of up to 1032m (3385ft). To get there, from the northeastern fringes of the city take the narrow ᴥ A 7000 country road, which runs through the park from south to north in the direction of Colmenar, and along its initial stages provides fine views back down to Málaga and the sea. Along the route there are turn-offs to the *Cortijo La Reina hotel (36 rooms | tel. 9 51 01 40 00 | hotelcortijolareina.com | Budget–Moderate)* and to the historic winery of *Lagar de Torrijos*, where a small trekking area begins.

NERJA

(127 D5) (ꝳ H5) Small beaches, a pleasant climate, attractive squares and atmospheric alleyways, plus splendid views of the coast and mountains – this is the appeal of Nerja (pop. 20,000) at the eastern end of the Costa del Sol.

Nerja has developed from a fishing village into an attractive little holiday town. Sure there are some new developments inland, but the local topography, with its cliffs and beaches enclosed by rocky headlands has prevented unbridled development along the coast. Locals putting boxes of fruit outside their front doors demonstrate that traditional Andalusia has not completely disappeared here: if you want to buy something, just ring the bell.

SIGHTSEEING

BALCÓN DE EUROPA ★ ● ᴥ
This is Nerja's showpiece, and together with the palm-lined promenade behind, it's a favourite spot for a stroll or for a rest on one of the benches. Spain's King Alfonso XII thought up the name 'Balcony of Europe' when he visited Nerja in 1885 and here, high above the water, took in all that sea air. Built on a vertical cliff and the remains of a hardly recognisable me-

dieval fortification, the Balcón de Europa provides one of the most beautiful viewpoints in Andalusia. There's a bronze

The Caves of Nerja house what must be Spain's most unusual concert hall

statue of Alfonso XII standing on his 'balcony', which separates the beaches of Calahonda and El Salón.

CUEVA DE NERJA ★

Stone cascades, curtains, throws, beads, columns – these are just some of the intriguing formations that will capture your imagination between the 'Hall of the Nativity' and the 'Hall of Phantoms'. Are they wrinkled old women, cacti, goblins, rats' heads in profile, the baleen of a whale, or organ pipes? The spectacular Caves of Nerja have all the many features typical of a dripstone cave, and this is a major tourist attraction on this part of the coast: each year at least half a million visitors come to explore the caverns, and in high season it can get very crowded. An auditorium has been built into one of the halls – in July it is the setting for a dance and music festival. Rediscovered in 1959, the caves were in use as long as 25,000 years ago. Today every nook and cranny is well lit. The caves lie to the east of the town, with the entrance to the car park well signposted. *July/Aug daily 10am–7.30pm, Sept–June 10am–2pm and 4–6.30pm | www.cueva denerja.es*

FOOD & DRINK

ANTICA ROMA

Good and atmospheric Italian restaurant, with an outdoor terrace overlooking the sea. *Daily | Calle Carabeo 12 | tel. 9 52 52 59 24 | Budget–Moderate*

REY ALFONSO ✄

This restaurant offers a feast for the eyes – the view out of the window! Considering the location right under the Balcón de Europa, the seafood and steak are quite reasonably priced. *Closed Wed in winter | Balcón de Europa (access from the end of the promenade) | tel. 9 52 52 09 58 | Moderate*

SHOPPING

Street markets are held in the Urbanización Flamingo every Tuesday and Sunday morning.

COSTA DEL SOL AROUND MÁLAGA

BEACHES

Nerja is distinctive for its mix of rocky coast and small beaches, including *La Caletilla* and *El Salón* to the west and *El Chorrillo* and *Carabeo* to the east of the Balcón de Europa. The largest beach, ☆ *Playa de Burriana,* lies further to the east: coarse-grained sand, some restaurants on the adjacent Paseo Marítimo Antonio Mercero, showers, children's play area, pedal boats, nice views inland and along the coast to the east.

SPORTS & ACTIVITIES

You can book diving courses with *Buceo Costa Nerja (Playa de Burriana | tel. 9 52 52 86 10 | www.nerjadiving.com).*

ENTERTAINMENT

Nerja's nightlife is centred on the Calle de la Gloria; bars for young people are to be found around *Plaza Tutti-Frutti*. There's a colourful programme of theatre, dance and concert performances at the *Centro Cultural Villa de Nerja (Calle Granada 45 | tel. 9 52 52 38 63).*

WHERE TO STAY

BALCÓN DE EUROPA ☆

Large high-rise hotel overlooking Playa de Caletilla and right next to the Balcón de Europa – what a location! *110 rooms | Paseo Balcón de Europa 1 | tel. 9 52 52 08 00 | www.hotelbalconeuropa. com | Expensive*

PLAZA CAVANA

Centrally located 3-star hotel with restaurant, small terrace and pool. *39 rooms | Plaza Cavana 10 | tel. 9 52 52 40 00 | www. hotelplazacavana.com | Moderate*

INFORMATION

Calle Carmen/Bajos del Ayuntamiento | tel. 9 52 52 15 31 | www.nerja.org

THE HEART OF THE STORM

'Se vende' – for sale: in recent times there have been more and more of these signs going up – on houses, apartments, pubs, restaurants and even yachts. But nobody wants to buy them. The economic crisis has cast a huge shadow over the hotel and restaurant trade and the region's property sector has been badly hit. Experts had long warned of the collapse of the property bubble but optimists thought the boom times would last forever. Shortsighted development, with no thought given to the state of the market, bred speculation. Ever more new settlements, *urbanizaciones*, were created, of-ten in neo-Moorish style (and of substandard material), and ever further from the saturated development along the coast. People invested in holiday homes costing three or four times what they were actually worth. More and more units were built but the prices couldn't keep on going up. The result has been bankruptcy, people desperately wanting to sell with no one to sell to, half-completed schemes and ghost developments. With their 'crisis prices' the Costa's pubs demonstrate the way back towards normality: blind greed is the first thing that has to go.

NERJA

WHERE TO GO

CALA DE MARO (127 D5) (*ⅠⅠ H5*)

This pleasant, approx. 200m-long sandy bay a good 5km (3mi) east of Nerja, provides an alternative to the town's beaches. It belongs to the neighbouring town of Maro, where a winding road is signed down to the car park.

CÓMPETA (127 D5) (*ⅠⅠ H5*)

It is a winding road indeed that leads up from the coast to Cómpeta (pop. 4000). Situated at an altitude of 630m (2066ft), some 20km (13mi) northwest of Nerja at the foot of the Sierra Tejeda and Sierra Almijara, it cultivates its image as a large white village and wine centre. The local dessert wine is called *Vino de Cómpeta*; the vineyards are spread across steep terraces surrounding the village. The mountains, the huddle of white houses tumbling down the slopes, the alleyways and the 37-m (121-ft) high tower of the Iglesia Parroquial make Cómpeta a quiet but attractive place. Life here carries on at a leisurely pace; funerals and weddings are major social events. You can get tapas and bottles of Cómpeta wine at the *Museo del Vino (closed Mon | Avenida Constitución | tel. 9 52 55 33 14 | Budget)*, a mixture of shop, bar and restaurant. *www.competa.es*

FRIGILIANA ★ ● ⌄⌄ (127 D5) (*ⅠⅠ H5*)

Spread across the foothills of the Sierra Tejeda and Sierra Almijara just 6km (4mi) north of Nerja, Frigiliana is a perfect example of a white village. A good place to start exploring is the Plaza del Ingenio, where the *El Ingenio sugar factory,* originally built as a mansion, still produces sugar cane syrup *(miel de caña)*. Frigiliana rises over several levels up to the pleasant square in front of the church of San Antonio. Typical of the alleyways are the hanging flowerpots, planters placed next to the entrances, looping electric cables, and the ubiquitous bougainvillea. Ceramic plates on the walls have pictures and text describing the fall of Frigiliana castle and other events from Moorish times. Information: *Cuesta del Apero 8 | tel. 9 52 53 42 61 | www.frigiliana.es*

Flower-filled alleyways and squares: the white village of Frigiliana

Three kilometres (2mi) outside the village on the road to Torrox lies ● ☀ INSIDER TIP *La Posada Morisca (12 rooms | Calle Loma de la Cruz | tel. 9 52 53 41 51 | www.laposadamorisca. com | Moderate),* a beautiful country house with a pool and lovely views over the olives groves and the sea. The turn-off is well signed — if you go for it you'll be opting for an oasis of tranquillity!

TORRE DEL MAR (127 D5) *(𝄞 H5)*

The extensive sunbathing areas, with sun loungers and parasols, are the main attraction of this rather sterile coastal resort 20km (13 mi) to the west of Málaga. The 2-km (1-mi) long beach with its coarse-grained black sand is called *Playa de Poniente.* Not far away and open from mid-June to the beginning of September is the *Aquapark Aquavelis (Urbanización El Tomillar | www.aquavelis.es). www. torredelmar.info*

TORRE-MOLINOS

(126 B6) *(𝄞 F6)* **A three-hour flight to Málaga airport, followed by a 10-minute transfer, and there you are, right in the centre of Torremolinos!**

Those coming here in summer generally know what they want. And it's certainly not culture! Fun, sun and alcohol is what it's all about, and there are more than enough bars where you can get tanked up before going off to the clubs and discos. Torremolinos (pop. 60,000) provides a holiday encounter for a diverse range of people, from gays to families to elderly couples. It is the archetypal package tour destination: with 50,000 beds, it prides itself on having 40 percent of the total capacity of the entire Costa del Sol. In view of this, its appearance is pretty much as you might expect, with large developments creating ugly scars on the landscape. Apart from the bars and discos, the touristic appeal of the town lies in its long and immaculate sandy beaches, its handsome promenades and some 300 Restaurants. It is much quieter outside the summer season.

SIGHTSEEING

CALLE SAN MIGUEL

This main thoroughfare is a pedestrian zone, the place for seeing and being seen.

LOW BUDGET

▶ In Nerja there's a selection of cheap guesthouses along *Calle Pintada,* including the *Hostal Plaza Cantarero (10 rooms | Nr. 117 | tel. 9 52 52 87 28 | www.hostalplazacantarero.com)* and the *Hostal Nerja Sol (21 rooms | Nr. 54 | tel. 9 52 52 21 21 | www.hostalner jasol.com).* In high season, you can get a double room for around 50 euros, in low season 30 euros.

▶ At Málaga airport buses will save the expensive cost of a taxi. The No. 19 will take you straight to the city (timetables at *www.emtmalaga.es).* Apart from that there are several direct connections to Marbella *(portillo. avanzabus.com).*

▶ In Antequera admission to the burial mounds is free!

▶ In Málaga admission to the Alcazaba and Castillo de Gibralfaro is free on Sunday after 2pm.

TORREMOLINOS

The range of leather bags, fashion jewellery, sunglasses and clothing is overwhelming; judge for yourself what is junk and what might actually be quite tasteful.

JARDÍN BOTÁNICO MOLINO DE INCA
Clear spring water, fountains, palm trees and water features – this botanical garden just north of the town is a veritable oasis. Mills were operating here even in Moorish times, and they were brought back into action in the 18th century. Today they are museum pieces and work with the push of a button. *Summer Tue–Sun 11.30am–1.30pm and 6–9pm, otherwise 10.30am–1.30pm and 4–6pm | Camino a los Manantiales*

PARQUE DE LA BATERÍA
The municipal park is distinctive for its large areas of lawn. There's a small lake with rowing boats and an ⚓ observation tower that can be climbed. Also: children's playground, fitness equipment, fountains, palm trees and plenty of benches. *May–Sept Mon 5–11pm, Tue–Su*

11am–11pm, Oct–April Mon 5–9pm, Tue–Sun 11am–9pm | Avenida del Carmelo

FOOD & DRINK

BODEGA QUITAPENAS
Sit right at the heart of things, and enjoy a meal of fried fish, sardines, squid and Málaga sweet wine, which comes straight from the barrel. Has a terraced area. *Daily | Calle Cuesta del Tajo 3 | tel. 9 52 38 62 44 | Budget*

EL BODEGÓN
This good French restaurant has been in business for over 40 years. The seats by the windows, which open out into the street, are especially popular. *Closed Sun | Calle Cauce 4 | tel. 9 52 38 20 12 | Moderate*

BEACHES

The plus points of Torremolinos are the 7km (4mi) of beach with extensive sunbathing areas and good infrastructure.

TURISMO RURAL

Adiós to the coastal bustle! It's up into the cool mountain air where it smells of pine and cork oaks spread their branches. For those who want to get away from it all, *Turismo rural* is now all the rage. Country hotels and holiday homes are oases of peace and make good bases for explorations off the beaten track; occasionally you might even get a swimming pool and lounge with fireplace. In the hotels, the owners focus on personal service while holiday homes are self-catered and available by the week or weekend. If you're looking

for a place in the mountains around the El Torcal de Antequera Nature Reserve, contact: *Asociación de Turismo Rural Sur de El Torcal (tel. 9 52 03 41 55 | www.tu rismorural-eltorcal.com)*. Depending on the season, houses for up to four people cost an average of 200–300 euros for a weekend, 400–500 euros for a week. For a rural holiday in the hinterland of Málaga and Nerja, contact: *Red Andaluza de Alojamientos Rurales (tel. 9 02 44 22 33 | www.raar.es)*, the association of owners of Andalusian farm and country homes.

The rise of the Costa del Sol began in the mid-20th century on the beaches of Torremolinos

Over the years, the former beach bars *(chiringuitos)* have transformed themselves into fancy restaurants. *Playa de la Carihuela* stretches away to the southwest, towards Benalmádena, and the main beach, *Playa del Bajondillo, points northeast towards* Málaga.

SPORTS & ACTIVITIES

Located in the northern part of Torremolinos and open from the end of May to the beginning of September are the *Aquapark (July/Aug daily 10am–7pm, otherwise 11am–6pm | www.aqualand. es)* and the *Crocodile Park* (see 'Travel with Kids' chapter).

ENTERTAINMENT

A popular area for going out in the evening is *Playa de los Álamo. A* gay scene centres on clubs such as *Passion (Avenida de Mallorca 18 | www.passiondisco.com)*. There's always a lot happening in and around Calle San Miguel, and the crowds ebb and flow until late at night.

WHERE TO STAY

GUADALUPE

This *hostal* is situated at the interface between town and beach and is therefore not for those in search of peace and quiet. All rooms en suite. *10 rooms | Calle del Peligro 15 | tel. 9 52 38 19 37 | www. hostalguadalupe.com | Budget*

MELIÁ COSTA DEL SOL

The great advantage of this double hotel block belonging to the famous Spanish chain is its location right on Playa del Bajondillo. Has two restaurants, swimming pool and thalassotherapy centre. Attractive online rates. *540 rooms | Paseo Marítimo 11 | tel. 9 02 14 44 40 | www. hotelmeliacostadelsol.com | Moderate*

INFORMATION

There are several information points, including one on *Plaza de las Comunidades Autónomas (tel. 9 52 37 19 09 | www.ayto-torremolinos.org)*.

THE COSTA DEL SOL AROUND MARBELLA

As artificial as the Botox-enhanced smart set relaxing in the marina of Puerto Banús, as natural as the stunning panoramas of beaches and mountains – in the western part of the Sun Coast contrasts and clichés converge.

The region is renowned for its many miles of wide sandy beaches, which have helped to make places like Estepona, Marbella and Fuengirola such appealing destinations. The flip side: in high season these very accessible beaches get completely packed. The busy A7 coast road and the parallel AP7 coastal motorway form a kind of boundary. If you're here on a beach holiday you shouldn't stay any further north than that.

In the distant hinterland, you can reach the dreamy village of Casares and magical Ronda. For something completely different, you can take an excursion to Gibraltar – a little piece of Britain hanging off the southern tip of Andalusia.

ESTEPONA

(125 E4) (∅ E6) **Estepona (pop. 66,000) began life back in the 16th century as a tiny settlement of 30 families. It has now developed into a fully-fledged holiday resort and yachting haven at the western end of the Costa del Sol.**

The modern tourism developments stand in sharp contrast to the attractive Old Town, with its lanes and chalk-white houses. Along the beach promenades fountains, bulbous street lamps, lawns

Photo: Puerto Banús marina

Beach fun, marinas and wild apes:
from the smart set on the coast to
picture-postcard white villages inland

and palm trees reflect the taste of the modern planners. You can see a long way from Estepona – Gibraltar and Africa looming in the distance, and the Sierra Bermeja rearing up behind.

PLAZA DE LAS FLORES

Orange trees, flowerbeds, fountains, cafés and benches make the 'Flower Square' the jewel of Estepona's Old Town. It isn't far from here to the church of *Nuestra Señora de los Remedios* dating from the 18th century, and the *Plaza del Reloj* with its araucaria trees and bandstand. In the surrounding neighbourhood life goes on as normal, with the occasional butane gas transporter squeezing its way through the narrow streets.

PUERTO DEPORTIVO

A slender little lighthouse marks the presence of the large marina, which has almost 450 berths. Here the yachting fraternity and nightlife scene converge

Behind Estepona, Casares straddles the hillside in the Sierra Bermeja

on bars, pubs and restaurants to suit every taste.

FOOD & DRINK

EL ARGANEO

Seafood restaurant at the marina, which serves, among other things, a mixed grilled seafood platter (*parrillada de mariscos*). Outdoor seating on the terrace. *Daily | tel. 9 52 80 14 42 | Moderate*

SIMONITO

A mix of traditional bar and restaurant with seafood and fish dishes. They also serve paella, but it needs to be ordered in advance. *Daily | Avenida San Lorenzo 40 | tel. 9 52 79 14 55 | Budget–Moderate*

BEACHES

The harbour moles jut out between the two long sections of well-kept beach – *Playa de la Rada* in the east and *Playa del Cristo* in the west. A few kilometres to the west of the town, everything is as nature intended at the nudist beach of *Costa Natura*.

SPORTS & ACTIVITIES

Diving courses can be booked with *Happy Diver's Club (Atalaya Park Hotel | Carretera de Cádiz km 168.5 | tel. 9 52 88 36 17 | www.happy-divers-marbella. com)*. To the west of the town is *Estepona Golf (Carretera de Cádiz km 150 | Arroyo Vaquero | tel. 9 52 93 76 05 | www.este ponagolf.com)*.

WHERE TO STAY

KEMPINSKI HOTEL BAHÍA ESTEPONA

One of several 5-star hotels in and around Estepona, the Kempinski leaves nothing to be desired. It has a lovely garden, large landscaped pool area and superb restaurants (*Expensive*). *133 rooms |*

Carretera de Cádiz km 159 | tel. 9 52 80 95 00 | www.kempinski.com | *Expensive*

HOSTAL LA MALAGUEÑA
In the Old Town, just a stone's throw from Plaza de las Flores. Inexpensive and simply furnished but all rooms have en suite. *16 rooms | Calle Raphael 1 | tel. 9 52 80 00 11 | www.hlmestepona.com | Budget*

INFORMATION
Avenida San Lorenzo 1 | tel. 9 52 80 20 02 | www.estepona.es

WHERE TO GO

BENAHAVÍS (125 E4) (*᠓ E6*)
Reached through eucalyptus groves and the gorge of the Río Guadalmina, Benahavís is 20km (13mi) northeast of Estepona. Although it doesn't have any sights as such, the village makes a nice enough impression around the Plaza de España. It prides itself on its large number of places to eat; the centrally located restaurant *Lindaraja Grill (closed Thu | tel. 9 52 85 55 65 | Moderate)* is geared to meat eaters. More than half of the 4000 people who live here are expats, including a large British contingent. *www.benahavis.es*

CASARES ★ (125 E4) (*᠓ D6*)
The ☖ winding road towards Casares (pop. 2000), 20km (13mi) to the west of Estepona, affords glimpses of this mountain village high above. Then, as you round the bend, it appears at close quarters: a sea of white houses. At the centre of the village is the Plaza de España with its fountain, *La Bodeguita de en Medio* restaurant *(closed Mon | tel. 9 52 89 40 36 | Budget–Moderate)* and a couple of bars.

Above the square, alleys lead up to the church and the ☖ castle ruins from where there are magnificent views of the mountainous surroundings. Despite the influx of visitors, Casares manages to retain an almost unspoilt village atmosphere. Clothes are aired in front of the houses, flowerpots hang on the window grills, and in the late evening the smell of food and the sound of TV waft through the alleyways. *www.casares.es*

GIBRALTAR (125 D5) (*᠓ D7*)
A limestone massif, 425m (1394ft) high, called The Rock for short, Gibraltar (pop.

★ **Casares**
Picturesque white village in the Estepona hinterland → p. 83

★ **Upper Rock Nature Reserve**
Join the wild Barbary apes on the Rock of Gibraltar → p. 84

★ **Teleférico Benalmádena**
Take the cable car up Mt Calamorro for a view of Africa → p. 87

★ **Puerto Deportivo in Benalmádena**
Colourful goings-on around the marina → p. 86

★ **Plaza de los Naranjos in Marbella**
Idyllic place to convene beneath the orange trees → p. 88

★ **Tajo Gorge in Ronda**
The gorge of the Río Guadalevín creates a spectacular cleft in one of Spain's most beautiful towns → p. 91

MARCO POLO HIGHLIGHTS

30,000) is a little bit of Britain at the southern tip of Andalusia. In 1704, the English stormed the rock, and much to the chagrin of Spain have never handed it back. This small area has *fish 'n' chip restaurants,* Royal Mail letterboxes and an approach road that curiously cuts right across the airport runway.

Spanish or British? Some of Gibraltar's inhabitants don't really care

Gibraltar, which lies 50km (31mi) south-west of Estepona, is worth a day trip, but watch out: car parks are few and far between and the queues when leaving can be very long indeed. It's best to leave your car in La Línea de la Concepción (charged parking) and cross the border on foot. On the other side, buses and taxis run to spots such as ☆ *Europa Point* at the southern end of the town, from where there are great views of the shipping in the Straits of Gibraltar and across to Morocco's Rif Mountains, their outline just discernible in the distance. And then it's up to the ★ ☆ *Upper Rock Nature Reserve;* the ticket includes visits to the small *St Michael's Cave,* the *Great Siege Tunnels,* which were dug into the

Rock during the Spanish-French siege of 1779–83, and the *Moorish Castle*. Along the way, you'll encounter Barbary apes, which like doing gymnastics on car roofs, defecating, and then pouncing on anything that looks like it might be food. Feeding the apes is strictly forbidden, on pain of a heavy fine! You can get up to the Upper Rock either by car (taxi if you don't have your own vehicle) or by ☆ *cable car;* there are more great views of the Gulf of Algeciras below.

The town's main shopping thoroughfare is *Main Street,* where many shops *(closed Sat pm and Sun)* sell alcohol, electronic goods, perfume and jewellery. But Gibraltar is by no means the bargain paradise it's sometimes cracked up to be. Some individual items might be a little cheaper, but not enough to make a trip to Gibraltar worthwhile for shopping alone. Though very nice, one trip to Gibraltar is probably enough. *www.gibraltarinfo.gi*

FUENGIROLA

(126 B6) *(ᗠ F6)* **Its Phoenician and Roman origins have long since disappeared under tons of concrete. In the 1960s its 8km (5mi) of long sandy beaches, with an average width of 40m/yds, propelled Fuengirola into the vanguard of mass tourism.**

Since then the number of hotel beds has risen to 12,000, and the population exploded to 70,000. Popular places to go include the large marina and Plaza de la Constitución. Walkers, joggers and cyclists share the beach promenade *(Paseo Marítimo),* which crosses the Río Fuengirola via a modern bridge on the south side of town. Playgrounds in the sand underline the family-friendliness of the beaches.

THE COSTA DEL SOL AROUND MARBELLA

SIGHTSEEING

CASTILLO SOHAIL

The rebuilt castle, which originally dates from medieval times, is perched on a green hill above the southern Ejido beach. The walls and towers also serve as the setting for various events during the summer, ranging from concerts to the *Mercado Medieval. Summer daily 9.30am–9pm, otherwise 10am–5pm/6.30pm/8pm*

FOOD & DRINK

AROMA

Mediterranean cuisine with fresh fish and meats, including some exotically spiced dishes. If it's too full here, there are plenty of alternatives on the same street. *Daily | Calle Moncayo 23 | tel. 9 52 66 55 02 | www.restaurantearoma. com | Moderate*

EL HIGUERÓN

Situated some 7km (4mi) to the north of Fuengirola, this is a classic among the Costa del Sol's restaurants. Andalusian cuisine (especially fish) is represented, as are dishes from northern Spain such as *fabada* (Asturian bean stew). *Daily | Carretera Benalmádena–Mijas km 3.1 | tel. 9 52 11 91 63 | www.elhigueron.com | Expensive*

MESÓN EL CANDIL

Small restaurant with rustic interior. The food is down to earth, whether it's the peppered steak or the grilled spare ribs. *Closed Mon lunch. | Calle Hernán Cortés 3 | tel. 9 52 47 86 44 | Budget–Moderate*

SPORTS & ACTIVITIES

There are boat tours from the marina, as well as diving excursions with *Abysub* (tel. 6 57 64 49 06 | www.abysub.com). In the centre there's a zoo that's open daily (Calle Camilo José Cela 6–8 | www.bio parcfuengirola.es). The *Aquapark* in Mijas-Costa *(end April–Sept daily 10am/10.30am–5.30pm/7pm | A7 km 209 | www.aquamijas.com)* is within easy reach.

ENTERTAINMENT

It all happens at the marina, at least in high season! Pubs, pizza parlours, cocktail bars and pubs provide evening entertainment. There are themed parties and live music in the *Mai Tai disco (Edificio El Puerto | www.discotecamaitai.es).*

WHERE TO STAY

LOS FAROLES

Bargain prices for the most basic needs – you'll hardly be able to find a cheaper pension than this one. People tend to congregate on the roof terrace, where you can also dry your washing. *15 rooms | Camino de Santiago 20 | tel. 9 52 46 22 97 | www.pensionlosfaroles.com | Budget*

FUENGIROLA BEACH

Aparthotel with 156 units, with either one or two bedrooms, kitchen and balcony. Also has a summer pool. It isn't right on the beach, as its name implies, but a couple of hundred metres away from the water. *Avenida de la Encarnación | tel. 9 51 06 27 00 | www.fuengiro labeach.com | Moderate*

LAS RAMPAS

A good 3-star hotel with restaurant and a small pool. The beaches and marina are within easy walking distance. *159 rooms | Calle Pintor Nogales | tel. 9 52 47 09 00 | www.hotellasrampas. com | Moderate*

FUENGIROLA

WHERE TO GO

BENALMÁDENA (126 B6) (𝄞 F6)
Benalmádena (pop. 60,000) is around
10km (6mi) northeast of Fuengirola,
spread out among the far-flung districts
of *Benalmádena Pueblo, Arroyo de la
Miel* and *Benalmádena Costa*. It is heavily developed and hopelessly confusing
but also has 9km (5.5mi) of beaches,
elegant beach promenades and plenty
of recreational facilities. With a modern
33-m (108-ft) high Buddhist temple
*(Estupa de la Iluminación | Paraje El Re-
tamar | www.stupabenalmadena.org)*,
the neo-Arabic *Castillo del Bil-Bil* (concerts, exhibitions) and right at the heart
of the community the *Torrequebrada
golf course (tel. 9 52 44 27 41 | www.golf
torrequebrada.com)*, Benalmádena
combines an interesting mix of attractions.

The focal point for the town's social
scene is the ★ *Puerto Deportivo,* which
is much more than your standard marina. With more than 1,000 berths, it is
one of the largest and most attractive
marinas on Spain's Mediterranean
coast. The whole place looks very artificial with building complexes in neo-
Moorish style, but it has a lot to offer
visitors. You can browse around the
yacht basins and jetties and there's a
great choice of shops, restaurants, pubs
and cafés. There are boat trips around
the harbour, boat services to Fuengirola,
sailing, little bridges strung with lan-
terns, boutiques, expensive ice cream
parlours, sangria by the litre, disco
rhythms and the *Sealife Aquarium (www.
visitsealife.com)*.

The *Parque de la Paloma,* with its paths
and ponds, is situated a short way inland.
Next to that is the not exactly cheap marine park of *Selwo Marina (mid-Feb–Dec
daily according to season 10am–
6pm/8pm/9pm/12am | www.selwo
marina.es)*. The highlights here are the
dolphin and sea lion shows, but there are
also penguins, pelicans, flamingos, igua-
nas and caimans. In addition, Be-

LOW BUDGET

▶ You can experience flamenco for
free every Wednesday from 12pm on
the ● *Plaza Virgen de la Peña* in *Mijas*
– provided it's not raining or stormy.

▶ In Marbella, there is free admission
to the cultural centre *Cortijo Miraflores
(Mon–Fri 9am–2.30pm and 5–9.30pm |
Avenida José Luis Morales y Marín)*,
which has interesting exhibits on its
18th-century oil mill origins. There is
also an archaeological exhibition.

▶ There is a combined tariff for
Selwo Aventura (see the 'Travel with
Kids' chapter), the marine park of
Selwo Marina and the *cable car from
Benalmádena*. Entry to the bird of
prey show *(exhibición de aves rapac-
es)* by the top terminus is included in
the cable car ticket. Check the times
at the bottom.

▶ Marbella is pricey, but you can get
an inexpensive night's sleep at the
Youth Hostel *(Albergue Juvenil |
Calle Trapiche 2 | tel. 9 51 27 03 01 |
www.reaj.com)* in one of the 210
beds spread across 69 rooms.
Open all year.

Built in neo-Moorish style, Benalmádena's marina has berths for 1000 boats

nalmádena has its own INSIDER TIP butterfly park *(just outside town next to the Buddhist temple)*, containing about 1500 specimens *(Mariposario | daily 10am–7pm | Avenida del Retamar www.mariposariodebenalmadena.com)*.

In the Arroyo de la Miel district there is a theme park, *Tivoli World (July–mid-Sept daily 5/6pm–1/2am, otherwise variable and sometimes only Sat/Sun | www.tivoli.es)* with a range of rides and amusements. Right next to it is the start of one of the best cable-car rides in the country – the 3km- (2mi-) long ★ ● *Teleférico Benalmádena (mid-Feb to beginning Jan, in high summer daily 11am–12am, otherwise according to season 11am–5pm/6pm/7pm | www.telefericobenalmadena.com)*. It takes just 15 minutes to get to the top of the 769-m (2,523-ft) ☼ *Monte Calamorro*, where paths lead off to various viewpoints. The coast spreads out below and in the distance you can see the outline of Africa. Impressive! Note, however, that in strong winds the cable car may not operate.

Accommodation options include the *Vistamar aparthotel (138 units | Camino de Gilabert | tel. 9 52 44 28 27 | www.hotel vistamar.com | Moderate–Expensive)* and the lovely *La Fonda hotel (28 rooms | Calle Santo Domingo de Guzmán 7 | tel. 9 52 56 90 47 | Moderate)*, which was designed by the Lanzarote architect César Manrique. Information in *Benalmádena Costa: Avenida Antonio Machado 10 | tel. 9 52 44 12 95 | www.benalmadena.com*

MIJAS (126 B6) (*∅ F6*)

The dazzling white of the houses, the neat alleyways and original architecture make this hillside village (pop. 3000) 8km (5mi) to the north of Fuengirola in the Sierra de Mijas an attractive destination for an excursion. Buses from the resorts ensure a stress-free journey. There are superb views of the coastal plain both from the ☼ garden next to the ruined Moorish castle in the upper village and the ☼ viewing terrace next to the *Santuario de la Virgen de la Peña*. This sanctuary has been carved out of the rock and contains an image of the Virgin with an interesting legend attached to it. In sharp contrast is the ridiculous spectacle of the 'donkey taxis', which stand around wait-

ing to give tourists a ride. Photos cost extra – it's a complete rip-off!

There are no peaceful, undiscovered corners in Mijas, but it has a pleasant enough atmosphere, and there are numerous souvenir shops, pubs and restaurants to explore. The small *bullring* is every bit as welcoming to visitors as the *Carromato de Max miniature museum (high summer daily 9am–10pm, otherwise very variable)*. Information: *Plaza Virgen de la Peña | tel. 9 52 58 90 34 | www.vivemijas.com*

MARBELLA

(125 F4) (*Ⓜ E6*) This overgrown beach town (pop. 130,000) still cultivates its reputation as an exclusive resort and celebrity haven – always that bit smarter and posher than elsewhere, whether it's the classy restaurants, the oversized conference centre, palm trees set in marble planters or the numerous golf courses nearby.

The flip side of the coin is the corruption scandal that shook Marbella to its foundations a few years ago, and its consequences. The local 'Mr Big' in charge of urban planning paid more than half of the town's councillors to flout planning laws, enabling him to earn millions out of new developments. The once-charming resort was soon carpeted in concrete. Interestingly, the very place where all this went on, the town hall square (Plaza de los Naranjos), remains the most beautiful bit of Marbella.

SIGHTSEEING

OLD TOWN

A criss-cross of alleyways, a few remnants of the old town wall and the ★ *Plaza de los Naranjos* comprise Marbella's Old Town. The square is a beautiful, colourful place with cafés and pubs, and, of course, the eponymous orange trees. In the middle of the square there's a bust of the Spanish king Juan Carlos I, and pigeons cool off in a fountain. In the southeast corner is the diminutive Ermita de Santiago, the town's oldest religious building, dating from the 15th century. It is the headquarters of the *Santo Cristo del Amor religious brotherhood*. Much larger is the nearby *Iglesia de Nuestra Señora de la Encarnación*, a cool escape during hot weather.

AVENIDA DEL MAR

Along this pedestrianised section of road, which turns off the beach promenade, you can admire the little INSIDER TIP *open-air gallery,* which has sculptures by Salvador Dalí (1904–1989). Works include 'Man on Dolphin', 'Don Quixote Seated', 'Cosmic Elephant' and 'Gala at the Window' featuring Dalí's wife and muse. A fountain and flowerbeds enhance the mini sculpture park.

MUSEO DEL BONSAI

For all fans of these miniature trees, the Bonsai museum has an impressive collection. *Daily 10.30am–1.30pm and 4–6.30pm (summer 5–8pm) | Parque Arroyo de la Represa*

WHERE TO START?

CITY **Plaza de los Naranjos**, 'Orange Tree Square', is the best place to soak up Marbella's Old Town atmosphere. The bus station is just outside town on Avenida del Trapiche; from there take bus L3 into the centre. Centrally located car parks include Parking Avenida del Mar, Parking de la Constitución and Parking Edificio Parquesol.

MUSEO DEL GRABADO ESPAÑOL CONTEMPORÁNEO

This art museum housed in the Renaissance building of the Hospital de Bazán has temporary exhibitions of engravings and art works by national artists. *Sum-*

DA BRUNO

This is a popular place from which to observe the activity along the promenade. Rice dishes, salads, home-made pasta. *Daily | Paseo Marítimo | tel. 9 52 90 33 18 | www.dabruno.com | Moderate*

Magical: Plaza de los Naranjos in Marbella, complete with orange trees

mer Mon and Sat 10am–2pm, Tue–Fri 10am–2pm and 6.30–11pm, otherwise Tue–Fr 9am–9pm | Calle Hospital de Bazán

PARQUE DE LA CONSTITUCIÓN

Small municipal park near the beach promenade, with cypresses, palm trees, banana plants and bamboo stands. It has a pleasant **INSIDER TIP** *park café*, where many locals meet.

FOOD & DRINK

ALTAMIRANO

Typical Spanish place with a loyal local clientele, serving only seafood – ultra fresh and ultra cheap. *Closed Wed | Plaza Altamirano 3 | tel. 9 52 82 49 32 | Budget*

BUENAVENTURA PLAZA

The pleasant little terrace on the church square is especially inviting. The menu changes according to season. *July/Aug closed at lunchtime | Plaza Iglesia de la Encarnación 5 | tel. 9 52 85 80 69 | www. demarbella.net | Expensive*

SHOPPING

Marbella fulfils its reputation as an exclusive place for shopping *(www.shopping-marbella.com)*. There's a good choice of boutiques selling international labels, including *Anika, Ermenegildo Zegna, Jackie Jean, Nota 90, Liberto* and *Loewe*, all of them to be found along *Avenida Ricardo Soriano*. The largest shopping centre is *Centro Comercial La Cañada*. Pu-

erto Banús is another option for those with a reasonable budget.

BEACHES

The marina separates the beaches within the town area. Parallel to the western beaches runs the *Paseo Marítimo*, a strolling promenade par excellence, which is also used by cyclists and inline-skaters.

SPORTS & ACTIVITIES

The *Funny Beach* go-karting track (N 340 km 184 | www.funnybeach.com) is located outside town on the N340. You can book diving courses with *Bucea en Marbella* (tel. 6 77 38 99 80 | www.buceaenmarbella. com), among others. Golf courses in the vicinity include *Los Naranjos* (Urbanización Nueva Andalucía | tel. 9 52 81 52 06 | www.losnaranjos.com) and *La Quinta* (Urbanización La Quinta Golf | tel. 9 52 76 23 90 | www.laquintagolf.com).

ENTERTAINMENT

A pleasant Old City atmosphere pervades the area around *Plaza de los Naranjos*. The marina is a popular place to meet up for cocktails, for example in the *Hestia* (www.hestiamarbella.com). The longstanding highlight of the Marbella nightlife scene is the Arabian-style and very exclusive *Olivia Valère nightclub* (Carretera de Istán km 0.8 | www.oliviavalere. com), which can accommodate more than 1000 people.

WHERE TO STAY

CASA LA CONCHA
A stylish bed & breakfast boutique hotel, off the beaten track. There are only five cottages, so book well in advance. Has garden and small pool. *Calle Jubrique 45 | Urbanización Rocío de Nagüeles | tel. 6 46 52 08 83 | www.casalaconcha.com | Expensive*

INSIDER TIP LA MORADA MÁS HERMOSA
Small and friendly, just like a country hotel – and in the heart of the Old Town. Some rooms have a balcony or small roof terrace. Rooms are well equipped and provide good value for money. *7 rooms | Calle Montenebros 16 a | tel. 9 52 92 44 67 | www.lamoradamas hermosa.com | Moderate*

INFORMATION

Glorieta de la Fontanilla | tel. 9 52 77 14 42 | www.marbellaexclusive.com

WHERE TO GO

PUERTO BANÚS ● (125 F4) (*M E6*)
Smart, smarter, smartest – Puerto Banús. In Marbella's neighbour 5km (3mi) to the southwest (boat services from and to Marbella marina), people like showing off what they have: deep wallets and low necklines, big cars and bigger yachts: this is where the wealthy elite tie up. The marina is one long catwalk – on which celebrities regularly make an appearance – and you'll see lots of killer heels, status handbags, little white dogs and expensive-looking jewellery, not to mention evidence of Botox and silicon. The marina is the perfect place to observe this fascinating scene, but it's also nice for an evening out. All around the harbour basin are restaurants, cocktail bars and boutiques generally catering to a very wealthy clientele. The 1km- (0.5mi-) long beach stretches east of the town, in the direction of Marbella. Behind the marina, there's more going on at the square named after the Hollywood actor Antonio Banderas, who was born in Málaga.

160m (524ft) over the abyss of the El Tajo gorge: Ronda's impressive location

RONDA (125 E3) (*E5*)

A visit to Ronda, situated around 60km (37mi) northwest of Marbella, is one of the highlights of a trip to Andalusia. The town (pop. 37,000) is perilously perched on a clifftop. Even the journey there along the A397 through the mountains of the Serranía de Ronda is an experience. The more than 100m- (330ft-) deep ★ ● *Tajo Gorge* divides the town. It is impressively spanned by the Puente Nuevo (New Bridge); at the bottom flows the Río Guadalevín.

'La Mina' is a **INSIDER TIP** secret passage with 200 steep and occasionally damp steps that lead down to the bottom of the gorge, beginning at the *Casa del Rey Moro (daily 10am–7pm | Cuesta de Santo Domingo)*. The Moors created the tunnel in the 14th century as a means of protecting the water supply in the event of a siege. Since 1912, the Casa del Rey Moro has been surrounded by 'hanging gardens', which reach down to the lip of the gorge, a little masterpiece created by the landscape architect Nicolas Forestier.

With its old town alleyways, the church of *Santa María la Mayor (Mon–Sat 10am–8pm, Sun 10am–12.30pm and 2–8pm)*, built over the former mosque, the Arab Baths *(Baños Árabes | Mon–Fri 10am–6pm, summer until 7pm, Sat/Sun 10am–3pm, Thu–Sat also 8–11pm)* and the Bullfighting Arena dating from 1785 *(Plaza de Toros | daily 10am–6pm, in summer until 8pm)*, there's plenty to discover in Ronda. A stroll across the Plaza de España and through the pedestrianised area around Carrera Espinel, as well as a walk in the small municipal park of *Alameda del Tajo* (especially nice is the ☼ terrace with views of the Sierra de Grazalema) round off a visit to the town. Stylish accommodation and food are provided by the ☼ *Parador (78 rooms | Plaza de España | tel. 9 52 87 75 00 | www.parador.es | Expensive)*, with the *Hotel Don Javier (12 rooms | Calle José Aparicio 6 | tel. 9 52 87 20 20 | www.hoteldonjavier.com | Moderate)* being a simpler alternative. Information: *Plaza de España 9 | tel. 9 52 87 12 72 | www.turismoderonda.es*

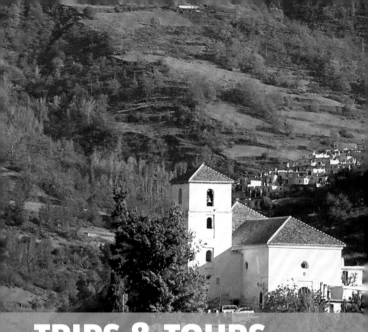

TRIPS & TOURS

The tours are marked in green in the road atlas,
pull-out map and on the back cover

1 THE MOUNTAIN VILLAGES OF THE ALPUJARRA ★

For this approx. 210km (130mi) round trip by car from Granada, it's best to plan an overnight stop, if possible in a rural hotel, farmhouse or guesthouse *(casa rural)*. Information and booking can be found at *www.ruralsierrasol.es* and *www.turismoalpujarra.com* as well as in the following tour. If you do decide to cover everything in one day, then be sure to get an early start. The most important stops are Lanjarón, Pampaneira, Capileira and Trevélez. If possible, avoid doing this trip on a Sunday when all the world and his wife seem to head for the Alpujarra.

Gorges, green river valleys, white villages looking like Cubist works of art – the mountain range of *La Alpujarra,* which squeezes between the southern slopes of the Sierra Nevada and the coastal mountains, is one of the most attractive areas of Andalusia. After the fall of Granada in 1492, many of the Moors expelled from the city came here. They have left behind a legacy of castle ruins, terraced fields and sophisticated irrigation systems.

The first stage of this route follows the A44 as far as the La Alpujarra/Lanjarón exit approx. 35km (22mi) from Granada. Turning onto the A348 country road, it plunges into a captivating mountainous landscape where olive, orange and almond trees flourish – even if the wind turbines near the start look a little out of place.

Photo: Capileira in the Alpujarra

Country idylls – even committed sunbathers on the Sunshine Coast sometimes find the mountains calling

The spa resort of **Lanjarón** is the first stop on the journey. You can pick up useful material from the *tourist information office (Avenida de Madrid | tel. 958 77 04 62 | www.lanjaron.es*. The shops of Lanjarón really capitalise on the village's role as the 'Gateway to the Alpujarra' – with pottery, dried figs, baskets, honey and pastries for sale. A short stroll will take you to *Plaza de la Constitución* and to the hidden *Plaza de Santa Ana*, a veritable botanic garden with its plethora of pot plants. In the lower village, take

a quick peek into the past and enjoy the fine mountain views at the 14th-century ☼ **INSIDER TIP** *Moorish hill castle*. The grounds of the little fort are freely accessible; the ruins themselves have been reinforced with steel.

Lanjarón is a long village that curls around the hillside. Beyond it, the winding road continues past olive groves and agave, fig and pomegranate trees. Shortly before Órgiva, which announces itself with its twin-towered church, the route turns left along the narrow A4132 to-

wards Pampaneira. Cacti grow right to the edge of the tarmac, as the road crosses the gorge of the Río Chico and passes the village of Carataunas. In the distance scattered houses cling to the slopes.

Beyond Pampaneira a detour leads via the elongated village of **Bubión** (note the artistic chimneys) for 4km (2.5mi) to ☼ **Capileira**, which between spring and autumn is a popular base for trekking in the Sierra Nevada. It sits at an altitude of

The village of Trevélez in the Alpujarra is the ham capital of Spain

● ☼ **Pampaneira** is one of the prettiest villages in the entire province of Granada. With its open-air cafés, souvenir shops and colourful woollen carpets for sale, it has long ceased to be a mountain hideaway, as evidenced by the large car park at the edge of the village. Narrow alleys, white facades, trickling fountains, colourful tile decorations, overhanging verandas, planters next to the doorways – everything looks pretty relaxed here despite all the visitors. Away from the main drag, on the church square, the *Restaurante Casa Julio (closed Mon in winter | Avenida de la Alpujarra 9 | tel. 9 58 76 33 22 | www. casa-julio.com | Budget)* is a good place to have something to eat; the emphasis is on hearty home-style cooking.

1420m (4659ft), and the air is already noticeably thinner here. The village is not as compact as Pampaneira, but it's enjoyable to stroll through the alleyways; there are several cafés along the rising main street. Capileira also offers accommodation, such as the **Hotel Rural Finca Los Llanos** *(40 rooms | tel. 9 58 76 30 71 | www.hotelfincalosllanos.com | Budget)*; the attached restaurant is open daily and serves specialities of the Alpujarra.

Back on the main road, attractive little villages dot the route towards Trevélez; first Pitres, then Pórtugos; between the two the road crosses the Río Bermejo. The next white village is Busquístar. From there, the road gets narrower as it negotiates gorges such as the Barranco de

Tesoro and Barranco de los Alisos. High above, clouds swirl among the summits of the Sierra Nevada, and you'll probably notice the temperature dip.

At an attitude of 1486m (4875ft), you finally arrive in **Trevélez**, its white houses covering the mountain slopes. Trevélez is split into an upper, middle and lower village. It is famous for two things: first as the highest village in Spain, as affirmed by a tiled sign on the way in, and second for the production of air-dried Serrano ham. The temperate mountain climate is ideal for the drying process; pork legs hang for months at the various small firms that have established themselves in and around the village. Most of the retail outlets are in the lower village; the aroma of the ham wafting onto the street provides temptation enough at least for a taster *(degustación)*.

In the upper village, the 12 **Apartamentos Siete Lagunas** *(tel. 958 85 87 26 | www.apartamentossietelagunas.com | Budget)* provide accommodation; in addition, a **campsite**, open all year, has an assortment of cabins to rent *(Camping Trevélez | tel. 958 85 87 35 | www.camp ingtrevelez.net | Budget)*. It gets especially lively in the village around the Festival of San Antonio celebrated on 13 June and the Festival of San Benito on 11 July.

Leaving Trevélez, the road crosses the Río Trevélez and continues through a succession of gorges, including the Barranco de los Castaños. Along this winding stretch of road, the mountains gradually recede; at workaday places like Juviles the way of life hasn't changed much in many years, with old men sitting together on benches and dogs dozing in the shade. If you're still looking for accommodation, try **Hotel Los Bércules** *(14 rooms | tel. 958 85 25 30 | www.hotelberchules.com | Budget)*, which has a restaurant and pool,

on the outskirts of the village of **Bérchules**, or the **Apartamentos Rurales El Vergel de Bérchules** *(Calle Baja de la Iglesia | tel. 958 85 26 08 | apartamentos-elvergeldeberchules.com | Budget)* in the village itself.

Beyond Bérchules, the easternmost point of the tour is reached. From here, the route runs via Cádiar and Torvizcón back to the A44; just beyond Torvizcón is the last panoramic view of the Sierra Nevada. Instead of going the same way back via Órgiva, follow the A346 until you hit the A44 at the impressive Rules Reservoir, at which point a more gentle landscape replaces the mountainous terrain. Back on the main road heading for Granada, you'll arrive at a pass called **Suspiro del Moro** (Sigh of the Moors), recalling the retreat of the last Moorish ruler Boabdil after the fall of Granada in 1492. It was from here that Boabdil is said to have looked down on his beloved Granada for the last time.

2 MYSTERY TOUR IN MAGICAL EL TORCAL

This 3km (2mi) walk through the ★ El Torcal de Antequera nature reserve is a great experience despite the brevity! You'll need a stout pair of shoes or boots and a car to reach the start and finish points – the car park at the visitors' centre, approximately 15km (9mi) south of Antequera. Bring water and a picnic, as there isn't much in the way of refreshments this side of Antequera. Recommended time for the walk: 1.5–2 hours.

What a magical place, with its mysterious rock formations of pinnacles, towers, jagged peaks, gigantic blocks and ridges! El Torcal de Antequera is Andalusia's most bizarre-looking nature reserve, a natural wonderland and geological curi-

Erosion created fantastic rock formations in the karst landscape of the El Torcal Nature Reserve

osity that has even been used as a location for science fiction films. The craggy limestone you see here today was originally on the seabed; movement of the earth's crust during the Tertiary period lifted it to its present altitude of between 1200–1400m (3900–4600ft) and then erosion by ice, wind and water over millions of years made it one of the most impressive karst landscapes in Europe. The Yellow Route (Ruta Amarilla), which partly follows the shorter Green Route (Ruta Verde), explores this strange environment. Wooden posts and yellow arrows mark the 3km (2mi) long route, beginning with the formations just beyond the car park, which resemble stacks of giant pancakes! The shapes inspire the imagination: there are grim-looking mountain sentinels, Indian chiefs in full headdress, sharks' fins and scaly crocodile skin. The crags are riddled with cracks and holes from which a variety of vegetation sprouts. If you are lucky, you might see ibex clambering over the rocks. Despite the apparently short length of the trail, you should allow plenty of time for the hike. It's difficult to walk and take in the landscape at the same time, and

you'll need to concentrate on where you're treading to avoid stumbling. Sometimes the route goes through narrow defiles. The small ascents and descents shouldn't be a problem for anyone who is reasonably fit.

After immersing yourself in this mysterious world, returning to the car park may come as a bit of a reality check. You can always pop in to the visitors' centre *(Centro de Visitantes | April–Oct daily 10am–7pm, Nov–March 10am–5pm | www.torcaldeantequera.com) to learn more about the reserve* or finish off by taking a short walk to the INSIDER TIP Las Ventanillas viewpoint.

3 ON TWO WHEELS IN THE CABO DE GATA NATURE RESERVE

For seasoned cyclists, this tour runs for 40km (25mi) through the Cabo de Gata Nature Reserve. It starts and finishes in San José → p. 41, where accommodation is available and bikes can be hired from companies such as Deportes Media Luna *(Calle del Puerto 7 | tel. 9 50 38 04 62 | www.deportes*

medialuna.com). **Don't forget to take plenty of drinking water, a repair kit, provisions and swimming gear – and adequate sun protection as it can get very hot! Although you're only going to be using minor roads, it's difficult to predict how much traffic there will be.**

It's no longer a secret that the Cabo de Gata Nature Reserve → p. 38 is a paradise for nature lovers. But instead of taking the dusty track southwest to the most beautiful beaches and the cape, take a bike tour in the opposite direction from San José. The route starts with a 3km (2mi) stretch to the village of El Pozo de los Frailes, where there is a replica of a historic waterwheel *(noria).* Just beyond El Pozo de los Frailes take the road on the right to Los Escullos (from here: 5km/3mi), Rodalquilar (10km/6.5mi) and Las Negras (17km/11mi). Thistles, prickly pears and agaves are the typical vegetation of the area.

The right turn leads you to Los Escullos, and the sturdy fortress of Castillo de San Felipe; it was built in the 18th century to guard against possible attacks from the sea. Just to the north of the little settlement is Playa del Arco, where you can stop for a cooling dip in the sea.

Back on the main road, you pass the white coastal village of La Isleta del Moro on the right, before arriving at the ☆ Mirador Las Amatistas from where there are beautiful panoramic views of the coast. Once over the next shoulder it's a steep descent (10 percent gradient) to the broad Valle de Rodalquilar. In Rodalquilar itself, the point on the tour that's furthest inland, you can pay a visit to the abandoned gold mines in the upper village.

The cul-de-sac village of Las Negras marks the turning point of the tour. It has its own stretch of beach, Cala del Cuervo, but it's probably better to stop for a swim on the ride back, perhaps at La Isleta del Moro, once you've got the tiring climb out of the Rodalquilar valley out of the way.

The tour follows the same route back to San José (via El Pozo de los Frailes); after Los Escullos those with mountain bikes can return via the coastal track, coming out beneath the watchtower that is visible from San José.

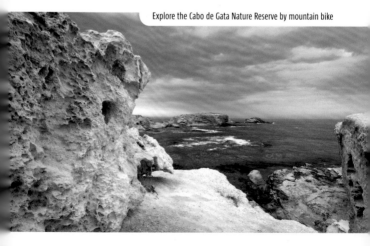

Explore the Cabo de Gata Nature Reserve by mountain bike

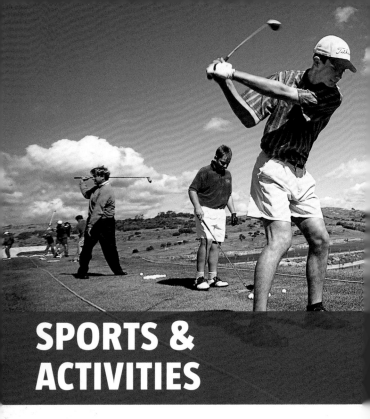

SPORTS & ACTIVITIES

Cycling and hiking, a round of golf, diving in crystal-clear water – every kind of sport and activity can be experienced on the Costa del Sol. And you'll even find free fitness apparatus on lots of the beaches and in many little villages, so there's no excuse not to work out during your stay .

CYCLING & MOUNTAINBIKING

Bike hire is not very common – because of the heavy development and traffic in many areas, the Costa del Sol is simply not that well suited to cycling. However, the Cabo de Gata Nature Reserve is a good place for bike excursions, while the mountainous Alpujarra will really test your fitness. In Spain, it is mandatory to wear a cycle helmet outside built up areas – and this is absolutely necessary because Spanish drivers generally have little consideration for cyclists.

Andalusia is well covered by cycling tour companies. *Andalucian Cycling Experience (tel. 952 184 042 | www.andaluciancycling experience.com)* operates from Monte corto in the Sierra de Grazalema west of Ronda and offers INSIDER TIP mountain biking holidays and road cycling trips as well as leisure cycling holidays and tough triathlon and winter training camps. *Biking Andalucia (tel.: 6 76 00 25 46 / www. bikingandalucia.com)*, a British company based in Órgiva, specialises in mountain biking in the Sierra Nevada and Alpujarra it offers a 7-day guided bike ride.

On land, on water or in the air: whatever you like doing, the coast and its hinterland provide plenty of activities all year round

DIVING

The best diving areas are the Cabo de Gata Nature Reserve, the Ensenada de las Entinas at Almerimar, the stretch between Castell de Ferro and Calahonda, La Herradura near Almuñécar and the coast from Benalmádena Costa to Marbella. Diving centres *(centros de buceo)* offer courses that comply with the regulations set down by the Federación Española de Actividades Subacuáticas *(www.fedas.es)*. The rocky coast of the Costa Tropical is a particularly popular base for diving schools, including *Buceo La Herradura (tel. 9 58 82 70 83 | www.buceolaherradura. com)* at the Marina del Este. *Isub (Calle Babor 3 | San José | tel. 9 50 38 00 04 | www.isubsanjose.com)* offers courses and access to the crystal-clear underwater world of the Cabo de Gata Nature Reserve.

GOLF

Costa del Sol equals 'Costa del Golf': that's how the Sun Coast markets its

many excellent golf courses. The area has long been a venue on the international golf circuit, with lots of high-profile tournaments staged here. There are more than 60 courses spread across Málaga province alone, which can make choosing one difficult (a good summary of each course can be found at *www.malagagolf.com*). Choose between courses with mountain or sea views, lakes, olive trees, tropical vegetation or spectacular water obstacles. High season is spring and autumn; in summer, you'll find lots of special offers available. Spain's own golfing legend Severiano Ballesteros, who sadly died in 2011, designed the course at ⚜ *Alhaurín Golf (Carretera Fuengirola–Coín km 15 | tel. 9 52 59 58 00 | www.alhauringolf.com)*, which has lovely views over the sea and the Sierra de Mijas. *Mijas Golf (Camino Viejo de Coín | Urbanización Mijas Golf | tel. 9 52 47 68 43 | www.mijasgolf.org)* comprises the two 18-hole courses of Los Olivos and Los Lagos. Golfing and hotel packages are ideal for players from overseas. A luxury complex such as the ● *Hotel Villa Padierna (tel. 9 52 88 91 50 | www.hotelvillapadierna.com)* in the Marbella hinterland boasts a wide range of spa facilities as well as INSIDER TIP access to three 18-hole courses, Located between Málaga and Torremolinos, the *Hotel Parador del Golf (tel. 9 52 38 12 55 | www.parador.es)* offers an 18-hole course and a golf school.

HIKING

The mountainous Sierra Nevada and Alpujarra are popular walking areas, but don't expect the kind of signing you get in the Alps. Information is available from numerous websites such as *www.turgranada.es*, from local tourist offices in places like Lanjarón and from the Andalusian climbing and hiking association *Federación Andaluza de Montañismo (www.fedamon.com)*. The Cabo de Gata Nature Reserve on the Almeria coast is a nice place to go walking. *Grupo J126 – Rutas de la Naturaleza (Avenida de San José 27 | tel. 9 50 38 02 99 | cabodegata-nijar.com)* offers guided walks of the area.

HORSERIDING

Riding schools offer one-to-one or group tuition – whether in single or multiple lessons (cheaper) – as well as treks into the countryside. They include the *Escuela de Arte Equestre Costa del Sol (Calle Río Padrón Alto | tel. 9 52 80 80 77 | www.escuela-ecuestre.com)* at Estepona and the *Club Hípico Los Caireles (Urbanización Lindasol | tel. 6 16 03 41 29 | www.loscaireles.es)* at Marbella. A number of companies offer riding holidays lasting from a weekend to a week. *Cabacci (tel. 6 69 22 66 57 | www.cabacci.com)* maintains stables at Guadix (Granada province) and San José in the Cabo de Gata Nature Reserve (Almería province), thus offering the choice of coast or mountains (or both).

LANGUAGE COURSES

Granada in particular has a long tradition of providing INSIDER TIP Spanish courses. There are courses for beginner and advanced students, and ranging from one week intensive courses to long-term courses lasting several months. Accommodation can be arranged on request Among the most reputable schools, accredited by the Spanish cultural organisation *Instituto Cervantes (eee.cervantes.es)* are *Castila (Aljibe del Gato 1 | tel. 9 58 20 58 63 | www.castila.es)* and *Carmen de las Cuevas (Cuesta de los Chinos 15 | tel. 9 58 22 10 62 | www.carmencuevas.com)*. Further information can be ob-

tained from the website of the Asociación Escuelas Español de Granada, *www.granadaspanish.org*. There are also a number of schools on the coast, including: *TC Languages (Plaza de la Fabriquilla, Edificio G | tel. 9 58 88 19 14 | www.tclanguages.com)* in Almuñécar on the Costa Tropical or the *Spanish Language Center (Avenida Ricardo Soriano 36, Edificio María III | tel. 9 52 90 15 76 | www.spanishlanguagec.com)* in Marbella on the Costa del Sol.

PARAGLIDING

A popular spot for paragliding *(parapente)* is the *Valle de Abdalajís,* a valley to the southwest of Antequera in Málaga province. The paragliding schools *Eolox (tel. 6 50 68 59 69 | www.parapentebiplaza.net)* and *Líjar Sur (tel. 6 17 49 05 00 | www.lijarsur.com)* specialise in tandem flights and courses lasting several days.

SKIING

Between November and March it's ski season in the Sierra Nevada. The ski resort of *Pradollano* lies between 2100m– 2,400m (6,900ft–7,900ft), with the highest ski lift and piste just below the summit of Mt Veleta (3398m/11,148ft). The resort has ski hire outlets, ski courses,

plenty of accommodation, restaurants, ski shops and room for thousands of cars at the Los Peñones car park alone. You can reach the resort by bus from Granada. At weekends, it can get very busy indeed, so it's advisable to book your hotel well in advance through the *Sierra Nevada central booking office (tel. 9 02 70 80 90 | sierranevada.es)*. Depending on the snow or lack of it, they may use snow cannons.

WIND- & KITESURFING

Because of the calmer conditions, wind-surfing and kitesurfing are not as popular on the Costa del Sol as they are, for example, on the Costa de la Luz, near Tarifa, and are offered only in certain places. On the Costa Tropical, *Windsurf La Herradura (Paseo Marítimo | tel. 9 58 64 01 43 | www.windsurflaherradura.com)* runs courses in La Herradura. On the Costa de Almería, *Sail & Surf (Playa Serena | tel. 6 59 04 77 92 | www.surfroquetas.com)* in Roquetas de Mar is a good place to try. For kiters, there's the *Freedom Kite School (Playa Guadalmansa | tel. 6 07 92 60 92 | www.kitesurfestepona.com)* in Estepona. The *Kite Surf Academy (tel. 6 20 31 44 21 | www.kiteboardacademy.com)* has no fixed base, but sets up at various spots along the western Costa del Sol.

The Costa del Sol and Costa Tropical are calmer than Tarifa on the Atlantic coast

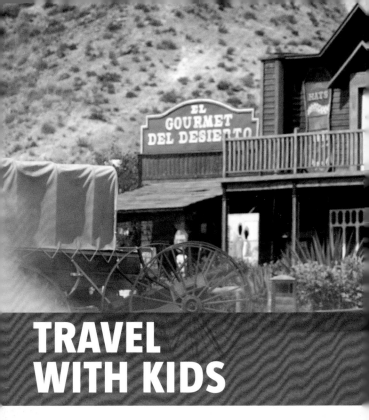

TRAVEL
WITH KIDS

Late to bed, a 10-week summer holiday and never being told to be quiet – Spanish children do quite well. The country is considered child-friendly, with most people happy to see children out and about even late at night.

ALMERÍA &
COSTA DE ALMERÍA

MARIO PARK (129 D6) (*M5*)
Kamikaze slide, Río Bravo, Black Hole – these and other attractions guarantee summer water fun at this Aqua Park in Roquetas de Mar. *Open mid-June to beginning Sept daily 11am–7pm | 21 euros, children (aged 4–12) 14 euros, after 3.30pm 14.50/10.50 euros | Camino de las Salinas | www.mariopark.com*

OASYS – PARQUE TEMÁTICO
DEL DESIERTO DE TABERNAS
(129 D5) (*M4*)
Good versus bad, a duel, a gallows, and stunts on horseback – the INSIDER TIP Wild West Show makes this Western film set, complete with saloon, bank and sheriff's office, really come alive. After all, this is where the likes of Clint Eastwood once trod the boardwalks. On top of that is the 'Desert Theme Park' with attractions ranging from a cactus garden, wagon museum and cancan show *(daily 1pm and 4pm, also at 7pm in summer)* to a cinema museum displaying film posters and ancient projectors. Most of the park is taken up by a zoo, with approx. 200 different species, including giraffes, rhinos and ostriches in a savannah habitat. Marmosets and leg

Pony rides and petting zoos no longer quite cut it. How about the Wild West, crocodiles, shark pools and an earthquake simulator?

hornbills live in the jungle house, and there's a parrot show at the little amphitheatre. The pool complex is open from June to beginning Sept (included in admission fee; don't forget swimming gear). *June–Sept daily 10am–9pm, April/May and Oct 10am–7pm, Nov–March irregular hours, mostly only Sat/Sun 10am–7pm, Western shows lasting 15 minutes at high noon and 5pm, also at 8pm in summer | 19.90 euros, children (aged 4–12) 9.90 euros, additional parking fee | N 340 km 464 | www.playasenator.com*

GRANADA & COSTA TROPICAL

ACUARIO DE ALMUÑÉCAR ●
(127 E5) (*Ø J5*)

Jellyfish and seahorses, coral, sea cucumbers and starfish are just a few examples of the sea-life here – this aquarium on Plaza Kuwait in Almuñécar might be small but it's very good. There's plenty to see and lots to learn about, from sole camouflaged in the sand to eels peering out of rock crevices. The highlight is the

'Oceanario' with its rays and sharks. *July/ Aug daily 10.30am–10pm, June Mon–Fri 10am–7.30pm, Sat/Sun 10.30am–9pm, Sept–May Mon–Fri 10am–8.30pm, Sat/*

Siesta on the beach?
Remember the sunscreen!

Sun 10.30am–7.30pm | 12 euros, children (aged 4–12) 9 euros | www.acuario almunecar.es

PARQUE DE LAS CIENCIAS
GRANADA ● (127 E3) (*ØØ J4*)

A tropical INSIDER**TIP** Butterfly House with butterflies *(mariposario tropical)* fluttering freely around, a planetarium, the 'Journey into the Human Body' pavilion: this educational but fun 'Science Park' will occupy children (and adults) for hours. The main focus is on the interactive exhibits, where kids can get inside a giant kaleidoscope and make electric circuits. Chemistry and geology are also explored (check out the earthquake simulator), while outside there are regular falconry displays. The main landmark

of the complex is the ☀️ viewing tower; at a height of 37m (121ft), the platform provides panoramic views of the city and the highest summits of the Sierra Nevada; if you look through the free telescopes in winter, you'll even see skiers on the pistes. *Tue–Sat 10am–7pm, Sun 10am–3pm | 6 euros, children up to 18 5 euros, Planetarium (programme usually only in Spanish) additional 2.50/2 euros | Avenida de la Ciencia | www.parquecien cias.com*

INSIDER**TIP** PARQUE ORNITOLÓGICO
LORO SEXI (127 E5) (*ØØ J5*)

Wild cries and shrieks will lead you to the Almuñécar Bird Park, occupying a sloping site sandwiched between the lower ramparts of the castle and a residential area. Steep pathways and steps lead between large cages dispersed around the site. There are some 200 species of bird, including parrots, cockatoos, peacocks and ibises, with descriptions in English and Spanish. But you don't need to read too much because it's all about admiring the gorgeous plumage of the birds, especially the Green and Hyacinth Macaws. Some of the species are threatened with extinction. Also of interest is the cactus garden, while the mountain views are a bonus. *Daily 11am–2pm and 6–9pm (winter 4–6pm) | 5 euros, children 3 euros | Plaza de Abderramán*

COSTA DEL SOL AROUND MÁLAGA

CROCODILE PARK 🚻 (126 B6) (*ØØ F6*)

Over 250 giant reptiles, from crocodiles to alligators, live at the Crocodile Park on the outskirts of Torremolinos. You can observe the beasts at close quarters in their open-air and indoor pools. The prize specimen is 'Big Daddy', all 1120lbs of him. He is always in the midst of a

small harem, and once lost part of his tail in a fight with a rival. It is well worth taking the INSIDER TIP guided tour, which is included in the price of the ticket *(usually daily at 11.30am, 1.30pm and 3.30pm)*. The tours (in English and Spanish) provide information on the characteristics and behaviour of the animals, which are sluggish on land but can strike in a split second. The offspring of these primordial, cold-blooded creatures are kept at the breeding centre. *June–Sept daily 10am–7pm, March–May and Oct 10am–6pm, Nov–Feb 10am–5pm | 14 euros, children (aged 4–12) 11 euros | Calle Cuba | www.crocodile-park.com*

COSTA DEL SOL AROUND MARBELLA

SELWO AVENTURA (126 E4) (𝄞 E6)

Half game enclosure and half zoo: 2000 animals live here, among the hills of the Sierra Bermeja. Travelling around on the 'safari trucks' kids will almost feel as though they're on a real safari. In the lakes area, Reserva de los Lagos, antelopes and gazelles leap around and elephants and giraffes have space in which to roam. There's lots of walking in Selwo Aventura, but it's not too far for the amazing INSIDER TIP bird canyon *Cañón de las Aves*. 340m (370yds) long and up to 25m (82ft) high, the canyon, in which several hundred birds live among the bamboo and gum trees in relative freedom, is covered in netting. Towards the middle of the canyon, where the path leads uphill, look out for marabou storks. At the entrance to the complex, there's an information panel detailing the starting times of the various shows (birds of prey, snakes). Activities such as archery and camel riding cost extra. *Mid-Feb to beginning Nov daily 10am–6pm (in summer till 7 or 8pm), Nov–Dec Sat/Sun*

10am–6pm | 24.50 euros, children (aged 3–9) 17 euros, parking fee extra | Las Lomas del Monte, sign for the turn-off at km165 on the A7 | www.selwo.es

The Crocodile Park is certainly no petting zoo

FESTIVALS & EVENTS

Folklore and fireworks at saints' festivals, pulsating sounds at music festivals – in Andalusia there's always an excuse for a loud party. The only exception is the sombre mood during Holy Week (Semana Santa) processions, when members of the numerous fraternities *(cofradías, hermandades)* carry religious statues on gigantic floats *(tronos)*, each of the hooded bearers taking a weight of around 54kg (120lbs).

PUBLIC HOLIDAYS

1 Jan: *Año Nuevo;* **6 Jan:** *Reyes Magos;* **28 Feb:** *Día de Andalucía;* **Maundy Thursday:** *Jueves Santo;* **Good Friday:** *Viernes Santo;* **1 May:** *Día del Trabajo;* **15 Aug:** *Asunción de Nuestra Señora;* **12 Oct:** *Día de la Hispanidad* (commemorating the discovery of America); **1 Nov:** *Todos los Santos;* **6 Dec:** *Día de la Constitución* (Constitution Day); **8 Dec:** *Inmaculada Concepción;* **25 Dec:** *Navidad.* If a holiday falls on a Sunday it is taken on the Monday.

FESTIVALS & EVENTS

JANUARY
2 Jan: ▶ ● *Fiesta de la Toma* in Granada commemorates the capture of the city by the Christian troops in 1492.

5 Jan: In the evening are the ▶ INSIDER TIP *Three Wise Men Processions (Cabalgatas de los Reyes Magos)* with decorated floats, music groups, the distribution of sweets and more, in Granada, Almería, Málaga and other places.

MARCH/APRIL
During Holy week *(Semana Santa)* ▶ *Penitential Processions* take place in many places, often going on for hours. Granada and Málaga each have more than 30 fraternities and just as many processions taking place between Palm Sunday and Easter Sunday. They reach a climax on Maundy Thursday and Good Friday.

MAY
3 May ▶ *Cruces de Mayo* ('Festival of the Cross') is a spring festival with lots of floral decoration in the streets, in Granada and elsewhere.

JUNE
Around 11 June: the ▶ *Feria de San Bernabé*, the festival of St Bernard, the patron saint of Marbella.

Fiesta fever: in one of the most fun-loving regions in Europe the decibel levels rise with every festival and celebration

END JUNE–MID-JULY

Towards the end of June is the start of the ▶ *Festival de Música y Danza in Granada* (www.granadafestival.org), with ballet and classical concerts at a variety of venues.

JULY

At the start of the month is the colourful ▶ *Feria* in Estepona, which lasts a week and incorporates a day fair and a night fair.

AUGUST

On the first Sunday of the month, thousands of people head for the INSIDER TIP 'New Year Festival' ▶ *Fiesta de 'Noche-vieja'* in the Alpujarra village of Bérchules. The reason for the unusual date: a power cut in the middle of New Year celebrations in the mid-1990s. Ever since then, to be on the safe side, New Year has been celebrated in the summer, and always with great enthusiasm.

15 Aug: in Cómpeta in the Nerja hinterland is the INSIDER TIP traditional wine festival of the ▶ *Noche del Vino*.

From around the middle of the month is the 10-day ▶ *Feria* in Málaga, accompanied by processions, concerts, flamenco, firework displays and bullfights. Further ▶ *festivals* take place in Antequera *(Real Feria de Agosto)* and Almería (concerts, bullfights, street theatre and firework displays).

SEPTEMBER

At the beginning of the month is the ▶ *'Day of the Tourist'* in Torremolinos, complete with procession, paella, horse and carriage displays; the ▶ *Feria* in Guadix, ▶ *Festival of Pedro Romero* in Ronda; and ▶ *Feria* of the local patron saint in Mijas.

▶ *Flamenco Festival* in the district of Albaicín in Granada.

OCTOBER

Around 10 Oct: ▶ *Feria* in Fuengirola.

LINKS, BLOGS, APPS & MORE

LINKS

▶ www.visitcostadelsol.com Website for Málaga province and the Costa del Sol covering a broad range of topics, with plenty of information about the sights as well as cultural and leisure activities on the coast and in the hinterland

▶ www.andalucia.com Well-established and very informative website covering a vast array of travel topics in the region, from flamenco classes to rural tourism, adventure sports to golf and festivals, and nightlife to flora & fauna

▶ www.theolivepress.es Website with news and articles of local interest with an extensive section on eating out

▶ www.surinenglish.com News website primarily of interest to expats

▶ www.andaluz.tv This site has news on Andalusia, with sections covering golf and the weather, and you can also click through the various webcams it has along the Costa del Sol

APPS

▶ Granada – Travel Guide minube Lots of tips on Granada created by the popular Spanish social network 'minube'

▶ Beaches of Costa del Sol Nothing has been left out: pictures, descriptions and GPS coordinates for the beaches of Málaga province

▶ NearestWiki GPS Identifies where you are and then sends you Wikipedia pages with all the background information on your current location

▶ Suntimer This app helps you calculate the length of time that you can lie in the sun without harm

▶ If you want to improve your Spanish using an app on your smart phone, Worldnomads, Rosetta Stone, L-Lingo, Lingvosoft are the brand names you'll come across. Take your pick!

Regardless of whether you are still preparing your trip or already on the Costa del Sol: these addresses will provide you with more information, videos and networks to make your holiday even more enjoyable

NETWORKS

▶ www.travelpod.com/s/blogs/Costa+del+Sol Reports, tips and experiences from the Travelpod Community. Expect to find the profound, the superficial, the hardly worth saying and the well worth knowing

▶ www.couchsurfing.org Describes itself as the largest traveller community. You don't have to sign up to find profiles of travellers or locals. Click 'Browse People' and then enter 'Marbella' or any number of Costa del Sol locations in the search field

BLOGS & FORUMS

▶ blog.andalucia.com Interesting range of subjects with constant new material. Linked to the andalucia.com website

▶ costablog.com Sports, property, fiestas, concerts, shopping – this forum has everything covered

▶ www.malagaweb.com/blog Useful blog focused on upcoming events

▶ www.expat-blog.com/en/destination/europe/spain/andalusia There is a large contingent of expatriate Brits on the Costa del Sol. Pictures, classified ads and a very lively forum. If you need specific information, then best to ask someone who lives there. It's also helpful if you're planning to relocate. There is another blog devoted to Málaga

VIDEOS & PODCASTS

▶ www.solchannel.com An enticing video guide to Costa del Sol, both for tourists and people who may want to relocate

▶ www.whatgranada.com Series of videos covering many aspects of the city and the Alhambra, plus online travel guide

▶ http://www.youtube.com/watch?v=koPgmHC-Cjc&feature=related Authentic takes from a flamenco show in Granada – not the best quality but provides a good idea of what to expect as a tourist

▶ www.360cities.net The 360° panoramic photos give an all-round view of top sights. Check out the views of the Alhambra, Málaga Cathedral, the Ronda bullfighting arena and many other attractions

TRAVEL TIPS

ACCOMMODATION

The choice ranges from the simple pension (*pensión*; even more simple is a *fonda*) to the guesthouse *(hostal)* to hotels, which are classified on a scale of one to five stars. Good information on camping is provided by the website *vay acamping.net*. Country hotels and boutique hotels in the cities can be booked through the *Rusticae* chain *(www.rusticae. es)*. You can find tips on rural accommodation *(turismo rural)* from *raar.es*; on villas in the Alpujarra region from *www. turismoalpujarra.com*, amongst others. Spanish hotel chains such as *Barceló (www.barcelo.com)* and *NH (www.nh-hotels.com)* cater to discerning guests.

Prices for accommodation in Spain are mostly quoted without breakfast; hotels rarely include breakfast in the price of a room. In any case, it's often cheaper and better to go to a nearby bar of café. Beware: occasionally prices quoted for accommodation exclude value added tax (IVA)

ADDRESSES

Spanish addresses are often not given a number, or are supplemented with '*sin número*', shortened to 's/n'. If this is the case, and you can't find the place you are seeking, ask a local. If a house number is followed by another number, this usually denotes the floor.

ARRIVAL

You should allow around two and a half to three days to get to Spain by car from the UK. The distances from London to Almería is 2300km (1500mi). The usual route is London–Paris–Marseille–Barcelona–València. Alternatively, take the ferry from Portsmouth to Bilbao/Santander and then drive down through Central Spain. You can download free route planners from the internet; they will not only help you plan the route but also to calculate the cost of the toll motorways in France and Spain.

The journey by train can take up to 30 hours involving several changes of train. The cost will be much more than the cost of a flight booked well in advance. *www.renfe.com; www.seat61.com*

Buses belonging to Eurolines *(www. eurolines.co.uk)* regularly travel to Andalusia from various English cities, with destinations including Granada, Málaga and Almería. Depending on the place of departure and the destination the journey can take between 35–40 hours.

RESPONSIBLE TRAVEL

It doesn't take a lot to be environmentally friendly whilst travelling. Don't just think about your carbon footprint whilst flying to and from your holiday destination but also about how you can protect nature and culture abroad. As a tourist it is especially important to respect nature, look out for local products, cycle instead of driving, save water and much more. If you would like to find out more about eco-tourism please visit: *www.ecotourism.org*

From arrival to weather

Your holiday from start to finish: the most important addresses and information for your trip to Costa del Sol

There are reductions for children, students and pensioners.

✈ The region's international airports are in Málaga (large) and Almería (small). Granada airport is an option for connecting flights from Madrid or Barcelona. There are numerous flights year-round, but the airline schedules change all the time. The Spanish airlines are not generally renowned for their service, and frequent delays, unannounced cancellations and lost or damaged luggage hasn't helped their reputation. It's best to check schedules and prices direct with the airlines: *Ryanair (www.ryanair.com), bmibaby (www.bmibaby.com)* and *easyJet (www.easyjet.com)* depart from various British cities for Almería and Málaga. *Iberia (www.iberia.com)* and *British Airways (www.britishairways.com)* also flies to Almeria und Málaga.

CAR HIRE

There's no shortage of places to hire a car, including at Málaga and Almería airports. However, hiring the car before you leave home is recommended; this not only guarantees availability but also costs much less. Weekly rates for a small model start at around 130 euros including unlimited mileage and fully comprehensive insurance, but the offers vary. Online agents such as *Auto Europe (www.auto-europe.co.uk)* or companies like *Centauro (www.centauro.net)* enable you to compare prices easily. Drivers have to be at least 21, but this may vary depending on the car hire company. The presentation of a credit/debit card is required. Watch out for financial pitfalls, which Spanish car hire companies like to hide!

They are obliged to mention their policy about filling the tank *(política de gasolina)* in their terms and conditions, but behind that lurk annoying and not insignificant costs. When customers take charge of a car they have to pay an additional, previously unmentioned, sum for a full tank, which, depending on the model, could be as much as 100 euros. You can return the car with an empty tank, but the sum you've already been charged is much more than the cost of filling the tank at a petrol station.

CURRENCY CONVERTER

£	€	€	£
1	1.10	1	0.90
3	3.30	3	2.70
5	5.50	5	4.50
13	14.30	13	11.70
40	44	40	36
75	82.50	75	67.50
120	132	120	108
250	275	250	225
500	550	500	450

$	€	€	$
1	0.70	1	1.40
3	2.10	3	4.20
5	3.50	5	7
13	9.10	13	18.20
40	28	40	56
75	52.50	75	105
120	84	120	168
250	175	250	350
500	350	500	700

For current exchange rates see www.xe.com

CLIMATE, WHEN TO GO

In high summer, the beaches of the Costa del Sol are often really packed. It's much more peaceful in the mild autumn and winter, though the sea water is mostly too cold for bathing from November onwards; between January and April water temperatures in the Mediterranean have a maximum of 15°C. (59°F). Autumn and spring are perfect times of the year for walking and cycling, as well as taking a city break in Granada with extended excursions. That way you will escape the intense summer heat, which reaches 40°C (104°F) in some places, and avoid the queues and the traffic jams.

CONSULATES & EMBASSIES

UK CONSULATE
Edificio Eurocom | Calle Mauricio Moro Pareto 2 | 29006 Málaga | tel. 9 02 10 93 56 | www.ukinspain.fco.gov.uk

US CONSUALTE
Edificio Lucio 1°-C | Avenida Juan Gómez Juanito 8 | 29640 Fuengirola | tel: 9 52 47 48 91| http://madrid.usembassy.gov

CUSTOMS

Within the EU, items for personal use can be taken in and out of the country. Although there are no limits on the amount of alcohol and tobacco one can bring in from EU countries, the following guidelines apply: 800 cigarettes and 10 litres of spirits.

DRIVING

The speed limits are: in urban areas 50 km/h (30 mph), on country roads – depending on the signing – 90 km/h (56 mph) and on motorways 120 km/h (75 mph). The maximum allowable blood alcohol level is 0.5 grams per litre. Vehicles may not be towed away privately after a breakdown; this can only be done by authorised towing companies. Drivers must also keep a high-visibility jacket in the car as well as two warning triangles. There is a distinction between toll motorways *(autopista)* and similar but toll-free highways *(autovía)*.

Unfortunately Spain has some of the worst accident rates in Europe. Nobody seems to pay much attention to pedestrian crossings. Keeping a safe distance from the car in front is a foreign concept and setting off on a red light is a habit that seems impossible to eradicate. If you're caught by the police for infringements such as using your mobile phone at the wheel or illegal parking, you'll have to pay an on-the-spot fine. And it doesn't necessarily stop there – you may find your vehicle being towed away without warning.

ELECTRICITY

Mains voltage is 230V. Remember to pack a universal adaptor.

EMERGENCIES

There is one number for all emergencies: *112*. The police are called *policía*, the fire brigade *bomberos*.

HEALTH

If you have a European Health Insurance Card (EHIC), you will be treated free of charge by doctors, outpatient clinics and hospitals, which are part of the Spanish Seguridad Social system. If you need to see a doctor, you should go to the local health centre *(centro de salud)*, though the doctors won't necessarily speak English, and dental treatment is not usually provided. Because of this, some holidaymakers prefer to see private English-

speaking doctors, a number of whom have settled on the Costa del Sol. A hospital's A&E department is called *emergencias*; the waiting times there can be very long and treatment doesn't always match expectations.

Anyone taking out private insurance should look at the small print, particularly that pertaining to cost reimbursement, for which you will require a detailed invoice *(factura)*. Chemists *(farmacias)* are everywhere, and are well supplied. Some medication is available without prescription, and some drugs are cheaper than at home.

IMMIGRATION

Identity card or passport is enough. If you're entering from a Schengen country there is usually no border control.

INFORMATION

SPANISH NATIONAL TOURISM OFFICES
Tourist information is available from the Spanish tourism offices and also at *www.spain.info*
– 6th Floor 64 North Row | London W1K 7DE | info.londres@tourspain.es
– 1395 Brickell Avenue, Suite 1130 | Miami, FL 33131 | oetmiami@tourspain.es
– 845 North Michigan Av, Suite 915-E | Chicago, IL 60611 | chicago@tourspain.es
– 8383 Wilshire Blvd., Suite 956 | Beverly Hills, CA 90211 | losangeles@tourspain.es
– 60 East 42nd Street, Suite 5300 (53rd Floor) | New York, NY 10165-0039 | nuevayork@tourspain.es
Information in Spain is available from the respective local tourist information offices *(oficina de turismo)*; however, you can't rely 100 percent on the accuracy of the material supplied, including addresses and opening times!

TOURISM WEBSITES
www.spain.info;
sierranevada.es;
www.almeria-turismo.org;
www.andalucia.org;
www.ctropical.org;
www.granadatur.com;
www.turgranada.es ;
www.turismodealmeria.org;
www.visitcostadelsol.com

INTERNET ACCESS & WI-FI

Many hotels offer their guests computer terminals and Wi-Fi, also known in Spanish as *wifi*. Whether it's free or not depends on the individual establishment. In public libraries, the use of internet terminals upon presentation of passport or identity card is usually free, but you have to expect delays and older equipment. Commercial internet centres are often connected to 'phone shops' *(locutorios)*. Prices vary, but as a rough guide 1–1.50 euros for 30 minutes is about right.

BUDGETING

Coffee	around 0.80 £ / 1.25 $ for a café solo
Petrol	around 1 £ / 1.60 $ for 1 l of unleaded
Bus travel	around 6.30 £ / 10 $ for 100 km
Lunch	from 6.30 £ / 10 $ for a daily special
Alhambra	11.30 £ / 17.50 $ admission charge
Souvenirs	from 2.15 £ / 5 $ for a small ceramic plate

MEDIA

There are more than 1000 different TV channels in Spain, including the main state-run channels TVE 1 and TVE 2 as well as the private Antena 3 and Tele 5. There are plenty of English-language channels as well, including BBC News 24 and CNN. English newspapers and magazines are available in the holiday resorts as well as in the larger towns, and, during the high season, the smaller ones. Regional newspapers such as 'Ideal' have useful information on events.

MONEY & CREDIT CARDS

Cash machines are widespread and major credit/debit cards such as Visa widely accepted. If paying by card, identification is occasionally required. Banks are usually open Mon to Fri from 9am to 2pm.

NUDE SUNBATHING

Topless sunbathing on the beach is widespread; completely nude sunbathing is allowed only on explicitly designated beaches *(playas naturistas)* such as Cantarriján on the Costa Tropical as well as remote beaches such as exist in the Cabo de Gata Nature Reserve.

OPENING HOURS

There are no fixed opening times for shops in Spain, but most are open Monday to Friday from 9.30am or 10am to 1.30pm or 2pm and from 4.30pm or 5pm to 8pm, Saturdays mornings only. In the holiday centres, many shops stay open right through the day and until late in the evening.

PHONE & MOBILE PHONE

To call abroad, dial the prefix 00, then the country code (UK 0044, US 001), the area/city code without the 'zero' and the subscriber number. The code for Spain is 0034, afterwards you should dial the complete number. Within Spain no area code is necessary.

Public telephone booths are best used with a phone card *(tarjeta telefónica)*, available for 5 or 10 euros from tobacconists. Mobile phones can be used without any difficulty; they always look for the network with the strongest frequency. If you want to phone a lot it's probably best to purchase a Spanish prepaid SIM card *(tarjeta prepagada)*, so you can save on roaming fees. In Spain expensive 'service numbers' begin with 901 or 902; mobile numbers with 6.

PHOTOGRAPHY

Memory cards and CDs tend to be more expensive in Spain, while branded batteries are often cheaper. Photography is forbidden in certain museums, such as the Museo Picasso in Málaga.

POST

Letters up to 20g and postcards take only a few days to reach other EU countries. Stamps *(sellos)* are available from post offices and tobacconists *(estancos)* which you can recognise from the 'Tabacos' sign. The cost of a stamp rises at the beginning of each year.

PRICES

Even though income levels are lower than in the UK and social benefits are fewer, the cost of living in Spain is about the same. Petrol, public transport and

services are, however, cheaper than in the UK, as is a glass of wine and tapas in a bar. The admission prices to sights and museums are between 2.50–4 euros. By contrast aquaparks and theme parks are expensive.

PUBLIC TRANSPORT

The bus network is excellent and the prices are amazingly low. Every largish town has its own bus station *(estación de autobuses)*. It's possible to travel the length of the Costa del Sol using commuter trains *(trenes de cercanías)* operated by the Spanish railway company Renfe *(www.renfe.com)*, which run between Málaga and Fuengirola. That way you will avoid the frequent traffic jams.

TAXI

Hailing a taxi on the street is not very common – it is more usual to go to a taxi rank or call one up. Taxis are pretty cheap at approx. 1 euro/km plus the starting fare of approx. 2 euros.

TIPPING

Satisfied customers at a restaurant generally leave a tip of between 5–10 percent; in bars and cafés it is usual to round up the amount at least a little. Hotel maids will be happy to receive 1 euro per day.

WEATHER IN MÁLAGA

	Jan	Feb	March	April	May	June	July	Aug	Sept	Oct	Nov	Dec
Daytime temperatures in °C/°F	16/61	17/63	18/64	21/70	23/73	27/81	29/84	29/84	27/81	23/73	19/66	17/63
Nighttime temperatures in °C/°F	8/46	9/48	11/52	13/55	16/61	19/66	21/70	22/72	20/68	16/61	12/54	9/48
Sunshine hours/day	6	6	6	8	10	11	11	11	9	7	6	5
Precipitation days/month	5	5	6	3	2	1	0	0	2	4	6	5
Water temperature in °C/°F	15/59	14/57	14/57	15/59	17/63	18/64	21/70	22/72	21/70	19/66	17/63	16/61

USEFUL PHRASES SPANISH

PRONUNCIATION

c	before 'e' and 'i' like 'th' in 'thin'
ch	as in English
g	before 'e' and 'i' like the 'ch' in Scottish 'loch'
gue, gui	like 'get', 'give'
que, qui	the 'u' is not spoken, i.e. 'ke', 'ki'
j	always like the 'ch' in Scottish 'loch'
ll	like 'lli' in 'million'; some speak it like 'y' in 'yet'
ñ	'nj'
z	like 'th' in 'thin'

IN BRIEF

Yes/No/Maybe	sí/no/quizás
Please/Thank you	por favor/gracias
Hello!/Goodbye!/See you	¡Hola!/¡Adiós!/¡Hasta luego!
Good morning!/afternoon!/ evening!/night!	¡Buenos días!/¡Buenos días!/¡Buenas tardes!/¡Buenas noches!
Excuse me, please!	¡Perdona!/¡Perdone!
May I ...?/Pardon?	¿Puedo ...?/¿Cómo dice?
My name is ...	Me llamo ...
What's your name?	¿Cómo se llama usted?/¿Cómo te llamas?
I'm from ...	Soy de ...
I would like to .../Have you got ...?	Querría .../¿Tiene usted ...?
How much is ...?	¿Cuánto cuesta ...?
I (don't) like that	Esto (no) me gusta.
good/bad/broken/doesn't work	bien/mal/roto/no funciona
too much/much/little/all/nothing	demasiado/mucho/poco/todo/nada
Help!/Attention!/Caution!	¡Socorro!/¡Atención!/¡Cuidado!
ambulance/police/fire brigade	ambulancia/policía/bomberos
May I take a photo here	¿Podría fotografiar aquí?

DATE & TIME

Monday/Tuesday/Wednesday	lunes/martes/miércoles
Thursday/Friday/Saturday	jueves/viernes/sábado
Sunday/working day/holiday	domingo/laborable/festivo
today/tomorrow/yesterday	hoy/mañana/ayer

¿Hablas español?

'Do you speak Spanish?' This guide will help you to say the basic words and phrases in Spanish.

hour/minute/second/moment	hora/minuto/segundo/momento
day/night/week/month/year	día/noche/semana/mes/año
now/immediately/before/after	ahora/enseguida/antes/después
What time is it?	¿Qué hora es?
It's three o'clock/It's half past three	Son las tres/Son las tres y media
a quarter to four/a quarter past four	cuatro menos cuarto/ cuatro y cuarto

TRAVEL

open/closed/opening times	abierto/cerrado/horario
entrance / exit	entrada/acceso salida
departure/arrival	salida/llegada
toilets/ladies/gentlemen	aseos/señoras/caballeros
free/occupied	libre/ocupado
(not) drinking water	agua (no) potable
Where is ...?/Where are ...?	¿Dónde está ...? /¿Dónde están ...?
left/right	izquierda/derecha
straight ahead/back	recto/atrás
close/far	cerca/lejos
traffic lights/corner/crossing	semáforo/esquina/cruce
bus/tram/U-underground/ taxi/cab	autobús/tranvía/metro/ taxi
bus stop/cab stand	parada/parada de taxis
parking lot/parking garage	parking/garaje
street map/map	plano de la ciudad/mapa
train station/harbour/airport	estación/puerto/aeropuerto
ferry/quay	transbordador/muelle
schedule/ticket/supplement	horario/billete/suplemento
single/return	sencillo/ida y vuelta
train/track/platform	tren/vía/andén
delay/strike	retraso/huelga
I would like to rent ...	Querría ... alquilar
a car/a bicycle/a boat	un coche/una bicicleta/un barco
petrol/gas station	gasolinera
petrol/gas / diesel	gasolina/diesel
breakdown/repair shop	avería/taller

FOOD & DRINK

Could you please book a table for tonight for four?	Resérvenos, por favor, una mesa para cuatro personas para hoy por la noche.
on the terrace/by the window	en la terraza/junto a la ventana

The menu, please/	¡El menú, por favor!
Could I please have ...?	¿Podría traerme ... por favor?
bottle/carafe/glass	botella/jarra/vaso
knife/fork/spoon	cuchillo/tenedor/cuchara
salt/pepper/sugar	sal/pimienta/azúcar
vinegar/oil/milk/cream/lemon	vinagre/aceite/leche/limón
cold/too salty/not cooked	frío/demasiado salado/sin hacer
with/without ice/sparkling	con/sin hielo/gas
vegetarian/allergy	vegetariano/vegetariana/alergía
May I have the bill, please?	Querría pagar, por favor.
bill/receipt/tip	cuenta/recibo/propina

SHOPPING

pharmacy/chemist	farmacia/droguería
baker/market	panadería/mercado
butcher/fishmonger	carnicería/pescadería
shopping centre/department store	centro comercial/grandes almacenes
shop/supermarket/kiosk	tienda/supermercado/quiosco
100 grammes/1 kilo	cien gramos/un kilo
expensive/cheap/price/more/less	caro/barato/precio/más/menos
organically grown	de cultivo ecológico

ACCOMMODATION

I have booked a room	He reservado una habitación.
Do you have any ... left?	¿Tiene todavía ...?
single room/double room	habitación individual/habitación doble
breakfast/half board/	desayuno/media pensión/
full board (American plan)	pensión completa
at the front/seafront/garden view	hacia delante/hacia el mar/hacia el jardín
shower/sit-down bath	ducha/baño
balcony/terrace	balcón/terraza
key/room card	llave/tarjeta
luggage/suitcase/bag	equipaje/maleta/bolso
swimming pool/spa/sauna	piscina/spa/sauna
soap/toilet paper/nappy (diaper)	jabón/papel higiénico/pañal
cot/high chair/nappy changing	cuna/trona/cambiar los pañales
deposit	anticipo/caución

BANKS, MONEY & CREDIT CARDS

bank/ATM/	banco/cajero automático/
pin code	número secreto
cash/credit card	en efectivo/tarjeta de crédito
bill/coin/change	billete/moneda/cambio

HEALTH

doctor/dentist/paediatrician	médico/dentista/pediatra
hospital/emergency clinic	hospital/urgencias
fever/pain/inflamed/injured	fiebre/dolor/inflamado/herido
diarrhoea/nausea/sunburn	diarrea/náusea/quemadura de sol
plaster/bandage/ointment/cream	tirita/vendaje/pomada/crema
pain reliever/tablet/suppository	calmante/comprimido/supositorio

POST, TELECOMMUNICATIONS & MEDIA

stamp/letter/postcard	sello/carta/postal
I need a landline phone card/	Necesito una tarjeta telefónica/
I'm looking for a prepaid card for my mobile	Busco una tarjeta prepago para mi móvil
Where can I find internet access?	¿Dónde encuentro un acceso a internet?
dial/connection/engaged	marcar/conexión/ocupado
socket/adapter/charger	enchufe/adaptador/cargador
computer/battery/	ordenador/batería/
rechargeable battery	batería recargable
e-mail address/at sign (@)	(dirección de) correo electrónico/arroba
internet address (URL)	dirección de internet
internet connection/wifi	conexión a internet/wifi
e-mail/file/print	archivo/imprimir

LEISURE, SPORTS & BEACH

beach/sunshade/lounger	playa/sombrilla/tumbona
low tide/high tide/current	marea baja/marea alta/corriente

NUMBERS

0	cero	14	catorce
1	un, uno, una	15	quince
2	dos	16	dieciséis
3	tres	17	diecisiete
4	cuatro	18	dieciocho
5	cinco	19	diecinueve
6	seis	20	veinte
7	siete	100	cien, ciento
8	ocho	200	doscientos, doscientas
9	nueve	1000	mil
10	diez	2000	dos mil
11	once	10 000	diez mil
12	doce	1/2	medio
13	trece	1/4	un cuarto

NOTES

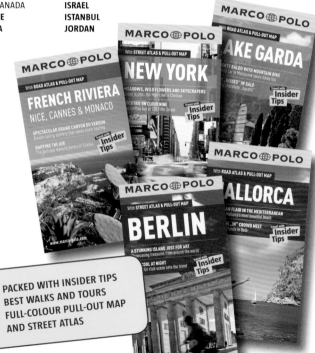

ROAD ATLAS

The green line [green] indicates the Trips & Tours (p. 92–97)
The blue line [blue] indicates The perfect route (p. 30–31)

All tours are also marked on the pull-out map

Photo: Frigiliana

Exploring Costa del Sol

The map on the back cover shows how the area has been sub-divided

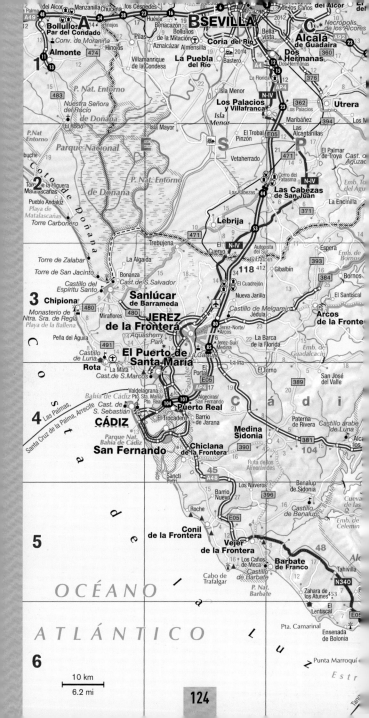

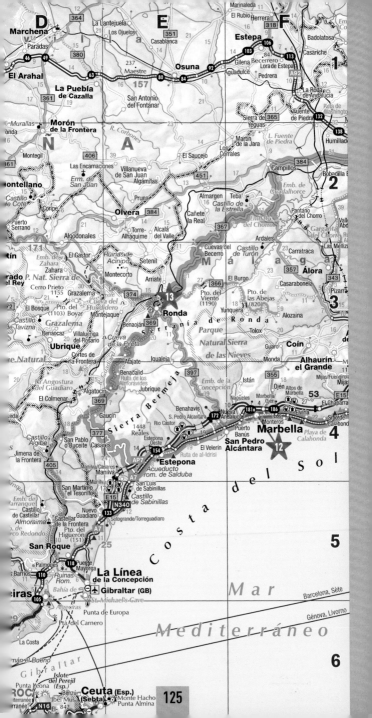

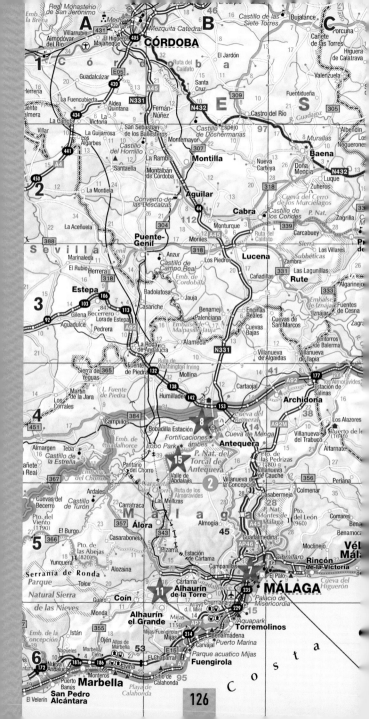

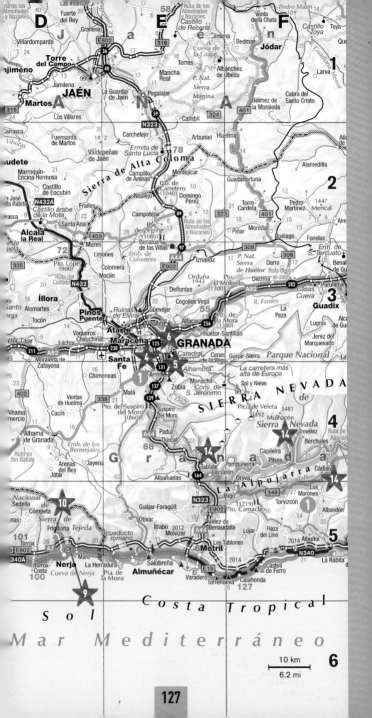

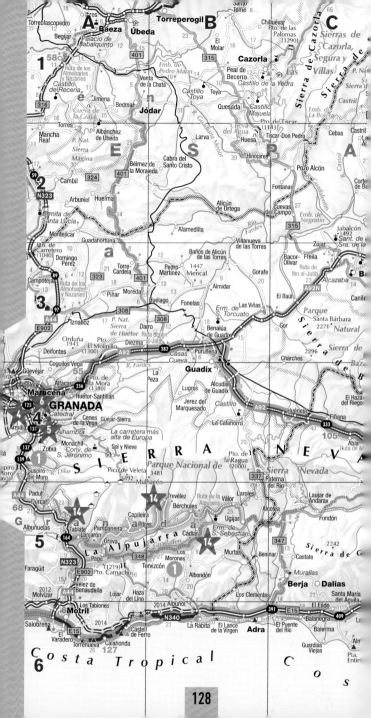

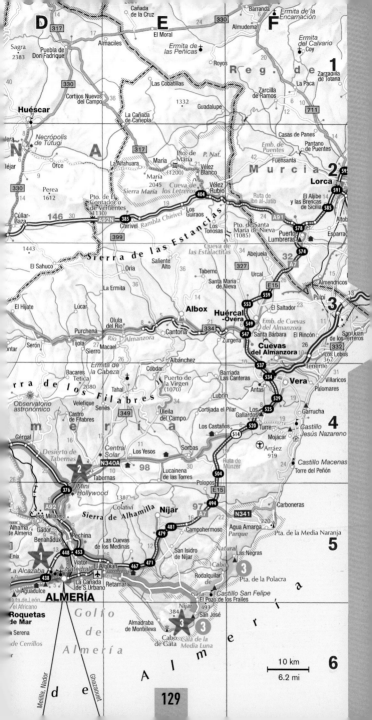

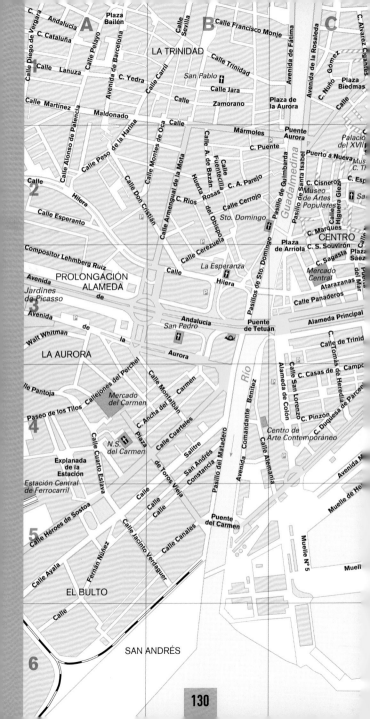

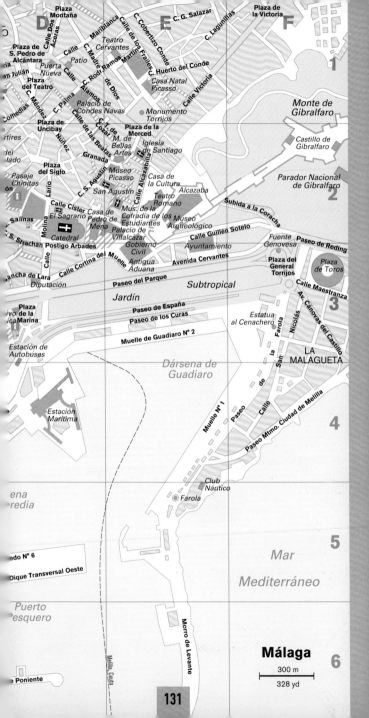

Málaga

300 m
328 yd

131

KEY TO ROAD ATLAS

Symbol	Description
18—26	Autobahn mit Anschlussstellen / Motorway with junctions
=====	Autobahn in Bau / Motorway under construction
I	Mautstelle / Toll station
O	Raststätte mit Übernachtung / Roadside restaurant and hotel
ⓧ	Raststätte / Roadside restaurant
ⓥ	Tankstelle / Filling-station
=====	Autobahnähnliche Schnellstraße mit Anschlussstelle / Dual carriage-way with motorway characteristics with junction
▬▬▬	Fernverkehrsstraße / Trunk road
▬▬▬	Durchgangsstraße / Thoroughfare
▬▬▬	Wichtige Hauptstraße / Important main road
▬▬▬	Hauptstraße / Main road
▬▬▬	Nebenstraße / Secondary road
▬▬▬	Eisenbahn / Railway
🚗	Autozug-Terminal / Car-loading terminal
▬▬▬	Zahnradbahn / Mountain railway
⊢○○○⊣	Kabinenschwebebahn / Aerial cableway
··········	Eisenbahnfähre / Railway ferry
�car	Autofähre / Car ferry
-------	Schifffahrtslinie / Shipping route
▬▬▬	Landschaftlich besonders schöne Strecke / Route with beautiful scenery
Alleenstr.	Touristenstraße / Tourist route
XI-V	Wintersperre / Closure in winter
× × × × ×	Straße für Kfz gesperrt / Road closed to motor traffic
8% ◄	Bedeutende Steigungen / Important gradients
🚐	Für Wohnwagen nicht empfehlenswert / Not recommended for caravans
🚐	Für Wohnwagen gesperrt / Closed for caravans
☀	Besonders schöner Ausblick / Important panoramic view

Symbol	Description
✳ Wartenstein / ✳ Umbalfälle	Sehenswert: Kultur - Natur / Of interest: culture - nature
〰	Badestrand / Bathing beach
☐☐	Nationalpark, Naturpark / National park, nature park
☐	Sperrgebiet / Prohibited area
⚲	Kirche / Church
⚱	Kloster / Monastery
♟	Schloss, Burg / Palace, castle
⚸	Moschee / Mosque
⚲ ⚱ ♟ ⚸	Ruinen / Ruins
⛌	Leuchtturm / Lighthouse
↓	Turm / Tower
∩	Höhle / Cave
∴	Ausgrabungsstätte / Archaeological excavation
▲	Jugendherberge / Youth hostel
♠	Allein stehendes Hotel / Isolated hotel
⌂	Berghütte / Refuge
▲	Campingplatz / Camping site
✈	Flughafen / Airport
✈	Regionalflughafen / Regional airport
⊕	Flugplatz / Airfield
▨▨▨	Staatsgrenze / National boundary
▨▨▨	Verwaltungsgrenze / Administrative boundary
⊖	Grenzkontrollstelle / Check-point
⊖	Grenzkontrollstelle mit Beschränkung / Check-point with restrictions
ROMA	Hauptstadt / Capital
VENÉZIA	Verwaltungssitz / Seat of the administration
▨	Ausflüge & Touren / Trips & Tours
▬	Perfekte Route / Perfect route
★1	MARCO POLO Highlight / MARCO POLO Highlight

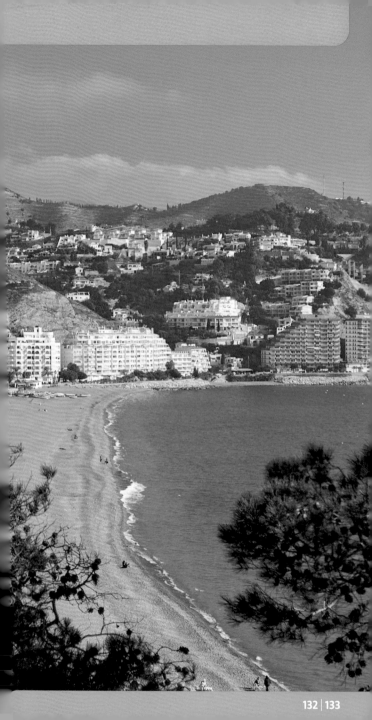

INDEX

The index lists all places, excursion destinations and beaches mentioned in this guide, as well as all the attractions and museums included for Granada. Numbers in bold indicate a main entry.

WRITE TO US

e-mail: info@marcopologuides.co.uk

Did you have a great holiday?
Is there something on your mind?
Whatever it is, let us know!
Whether you want to praise, alert us
to errors or give us a personal tip –
MARCO POLO would be pleased to
hear from you.
We do everything we can to provide the
very latest information for your trip.

Nevertheless, despite all of our authors'
thorough research, errors can creep in.
MARCO POLO does not accept any
liability for this. Please contact us by
e-mail or post.

MARCO POLO Travel Publishing Ltd
Pinewood, Chineham Business Park
Crockford Lane, Chineham
Basingstoke, Hampshire RG24 8AL
United Kingdom

PICTURE CREDITS

Cover Photograph: Nerja (Look: age fotostock)
Images: BioNatura (16 top); A. Drouve (1 bottom); DuMont Bildarchiv: Gonzalez (flap l., 2 centre bottom, 20, 32/33, 63); FIND DE LUXE VINTAGE (17 top); R. Gerth (108 top); Huber: Gräfenhain (3 top, 64/65, 122/123), Ripani (7, 50), Schmid (34), Stadler (2 bottom, 44/45); ©iStockphoto.com: Shaun Dodds (17 bottom); Laif: Gonzalez (3 bottom, 26 l., 28, 28/29, 29, 53, 57, 59, 60, 84, 91, 92/93, 94, 98/99, 106/107, 107, 109), Modrow (18/19), Tophoven (15, 22, 24/25, 96, 101); Laif/Hemis.fr: Gardel (54); Look: age fotostock (flap r., 1 top, 3 centre, 30 r., 39, 42/43, 71, 80/81, 87), Pompe (12/13), Richter (40), Stumpe (69); R. Lueger (2 centre top, 6, 76); mauritius images: Alamy (2 top, 4, 5, 9, 10/11, 26 r., 27, 30 l., 37, 74, 82, 89, 97, 102/103, 105, 108 bottom), Mattes (8); Ociosport Eventos y Aventuras p. L. (16 centre); Purobeach (16 bottom); D. Renckhoff (49, 66); K. Thiele (46, 79); H. Wagner (106); White Star: Gumm (73); T. P. Widmann (104)

1st Edition 2013

Worldwide Distribution: Marco Polo Travel Publishing Ltd, Pinewood, Chineham Business Park, Crockford Lane, Basingstoke, Hampshire RG24 8AL, United Kingdom. Email: sales@marcopolouk.com
© MAIRDUMONT GmbH & Co. KG, Ostfildern
Chief editors: Michaela Lienemann (concept, managing editor), Marion Zorn (concept, text editor)
Author: Andreas Drouve, Editor: Nikolai Michaelis
Programme supervision: Anita Dahlinger, Ann-Katrin Kutzner, Nikolai Michaelis
Picture editor: Gabriele Forst; What's hot: wunder media, Munich;
Cartography road atlas: © MAIRDUMONT, Ostfildern; Cartography pull-out map: © MAIRDUMONT, Ostfildern
Design: milchhof : atelier, Berlin; Front cover, pull-out map cover, page 1: factor product munich
Translated from German by Tony Halliday, Oxford; editor of the English edition: Dorothy Stannard, London
Prepress: BW-Medien GmbH, Leonberg
Phrase book in cooperation with Ernst Klett Sprachen GmbH, Stuttgart, Editorial by Pons Wörterbücher

DOS & DON'TS 👆

A few things to bear in mind on the Costa del Sol

DO WATCH OUT ON THE ROUNDABOUTS

Roundabouts can be a real traffic nightmare. When locals want to turn off, they will suddenly cut across from the inside lane (the fast lane) to the outside lane to take the next exit to the right – without care and without indicating. You really have to watch out.

DON'T TAKE TIME TOO LITERALLY

Andalusians have a relaxed approach to life and hate being time slaves. If you've arranged to meet a local, be prepared for the possibility he/she might be late. With agreements and promises, don't assume they will happen on time, or even that they will happen at all.

DON'T GET STUCK

In some mountain villages, the alleyways might suddenly narrow without any warning, thereby posing potential problems for unsuspecting drivers. It's best to leave your vehicle in the lower village and walk the rest of the way. Much less stressful!

DON'T GO TO THE WRONG 'CLUB'

The word 'club' sounds innocuous enough – it must surely be a sports club or a nightclub. Not so! In most cases in Spain a club is a brothel. In the evening 'club' lights flash on the roads out of town.

DON'T CLAP ALONG TO FLAMENCO

While some shows have a commercial character, flamenco is first and foremost an art form: the dance, the music, the whole spectacle. Accompaniments include finger snapping and rhythmic handclapping – but only on the part of the performers! Anyone who claps along to flamenco is making a real faux pas.

DON'T BE TOO RECKLESS

You should beware of theft almost everywhere. In Granada, be wary of women who try to sell you little bunches of herbs, and after dark avoid isolated areas in the Albaicín and Sacromonte. Car thieves are busy everywhere. You shouldn't leave anything visible inside the car – that's anything! Not even a biro, a map or sunglasses.

DON'T MISCALCULATE COSTS

If you tot everything up in advance, you need to know that in some hotels and restaurants the prices given exclude 8 percent value-added tax *(IVA)*. If in doubt, ask beforehand whether the tax is included *(IVA incluido)* or not.